New Folk Devils
Muslim boys and education in England

New Folk Devils
Muslim boys and education in England

Farzana Shain

Trentham Books

Stoke on Trent, UK and Sterling, USA

Trentham Books Limited
Westview House   22883 Quicksilver Drive
734 London Road   Sterling
Oakhill   VA 20166-2012
Stoke on Trent   USA
Staffordshire
England ST4 5NP

First published 2011

British Library Cataloguing-in-Publication Data
A catalogue record for this book is available from the British Library

ISBN: 978 1 85856 442 5

Designed and typeset by Trentham Books Ltd
Printed and bound in Great Britain by 4edge Limited, Hockley.

For Pinnu and Ragia

Contents

Acknowledgments

I wish to thank all the staff and students across the schools and youth group who gave up valuable time to be involved in the research. Thanks are also due to Ken Jones and Nafsika Alexiadou for reading and commenting on parts of the text – the usual disclaimer applies – and to Gillian Klein at Trentham who has been amazingly supportive and patient (again!). I am especially grateful to Rokhsana Shain for taking a great cover picture and to Ehsan Shah, Noman Javed, Usman Azar for agreeing to be in it.

Huge thanks to my fantastically supportive family – sorry for seeing so little of you all towards the end of writing this book.

To Bulent, Ada, Leyla and Saira – thank you for everything.

Key for text analysis

[ ]	word replaced to clarify meaning
[....]	extraneous material removed
...	short pause
......	long pause
????	inaudible
***	different interview
- - -	another excerpt from the same interview

Introduction

Since the mid 1980s, Muslim youth in England, especially boys and young men of Pakistani and Bangladeshi origin, have come to occupy the status of a new 'folk devil' or what Cohen (2002:2) refers to as 'visible reminders of what we should not be'. A group that was once regarded as passive and law-abiding, especially when compared with their African-Caribbean counterparts has, since the 1980s, been firmly recast in the public imagination as a threat to the social order. While statistics (DfES, 2007a) show them to be among the losers in the achievement game, Pakistani and Bangladeshi boys have not been the focus of concerns about underachievement in the same way that boys in general have. Instead, discourses of self-segregation (Cantle, 2001; Ousley, 2001; Denham, 2002) and global (in)security posed by the 'war on terror' have positioned them simultaneously as the victims of cultural and religious practices and as a threat to the social order.

Public and political anxieties about radicalisation and 'extremism' – already in circulation from the late 1980s – intensified to a point of frenzy after the London transport bombings in July 2005 were attributed to 'home-grown' suicide-bombers. Since then, Muslim communities have come under unprecedented scrutiny and surveillance at the same time as their loyalty to the British state has been significantly questioned.

Fears about Muslim extremism have intersected with national and European level discourses of integration. For example, in 2010, fierce debate erupted in Europe following the publication of German ex-banker Thilo Sarrazin's book about the impact of 'Muslim' (specifically Turkish) immigration on German nationhood. The book, *Germany Does Away with Itself*, suggested that the declining economic power of Germany was inextricably linked to the presence in that country of a Muslim 'under-class'. He asserted that this Muslim population is under educated, over populated (they have large families), and prone to crime. Although the book provoked outrage, I suggest in chapter one that its main arguments do not depart significantly from those already institutionalised by governments across Western nations in relation to, for example, Lebanese immigrants in Australia, North Africans in France and Turks in Holland.

In England, a mainly Pakistani and Bangladeshi population has been the subject of integration discourses. The *Community Cohesion* agenda was born out of the official government response (Cantle, 2001; Ousley, 2001; Denham, 2002) to the inner-city disturbances that took place across Bradford, Oldham, Burnley and Stoke-on-Trent in the spring and summer of 2001. The now infamous slogans of 'parallel lives' and 'self-segregation' (*ibid*) have come to characterise and symbolise a pre-dominantly Pakistani and Bangladeshi community under extreme pressure and nearing meltdown – and one that is read through current policy discourses of choice (self-segregation) and insularity (refusing to integrate into a British way of life or rejecting citizenship), as respon-sible for its own marginality.

As Clare Alexander (2004) has argued, the demonisation of Muslim Asians in England is inseparable from the notion of cultural community breakdown in which the perceived patriarchal authority of the family is seen as fractured, leading to underachievement and high levels of un-employment. This cultural pathology argument, which was drawn on in official explanations of the disturbances in 2001, feeds into wider con-cerns about working class young men (McDowell, 2002; Nayak, 2003) but resonates especially with long-established racialised debates about young black men.

Gendered, racialised and heterosexual discourses currently portray Muslim and Asian boys as part of hyper-masculine Asian gangs who are out of control and out of touch with British norms and values. Rela-tionally, girls continue to be positioned as passive victims of patriarchal cultures that oppress them. These newly constructed images of vio-lence and terror overshadow previously dominant but still present stereotypes of studious and passive Asian masculinity (see, for example,

Tanwar in *EastEnders*). Even the rare positive portrayals of Muslim men such as Amir Khan (discussed in chapter one) are also often used to reinforce pathological readings of the majority of young working class Muslim boys as disaffected and facing a future of terrorism or violent criminality (Burdsey, 2007).

Folk devils

For generations, young white working class men have been the focus of adult anxieties and fears, particularly in periods of economic crisis and social change in England (Pearson, 1983; Hebdige, 1979). A range of anti-heroes (Delamont, 2000) or folk devils has graced the public imagination over the last 50 years, including Mods, Rockers, skinheads, muggers, hoodies, chavs and Asian gangs. Pearson (1983) traces a long history, going back to the seventeenth century, of moral campaigners and political figures, comparing the yobs of today with a more disciplined, idealised youth of yesteryear.

The term folk devil, now part of everyday language, was aptly applied by Clare Alexander (2000) in her excellent ethnography, *The Asian Gang*, to the newfound status of Muslim Asian boys as society's scapegoats. The term originates in Stan Cohen's seminal work, *Folk Devils and Moral Panics* (2002). He applied it to a group of Mods and Rockers who, in the 1960s and 1970s, became scapegoated as the symbols of society's ills. Through a spiralling sequence of media reports, public letters and public reactions, they came to be represented as a 'threat to the nation'.

The concept of folk devil needs to be read in interaction with the notion of moral panic. Cohen defines moral panic as follows:

> A condition, episode, person or groups of persons emerges to become defined as a threat to societal values and interests; its nature is presented in a stylized and stereotypical fashion by the mass media; the moral barricades are manned by editors, bishops, politicians and other right-thinking people; socially accredited experts pronounce their diagnoses and solutions; ways of coping are evolved (or more often) resorted to; the condition then disappears, submerges or deteriorates and becomes more visible. (Cohen, 2002:9)

The concept of moral panic has been critiqued, evaluated and re-assessed by researchers, including Cohen himself, in the light of new concepts and theories (see Garland, 2008 for a review). Jefferson (2008) argues that Cohen's original definition answered the *what* and *who* questions but the not the *why*: that is, why moral panics take root around particular folk devils in particular societies at particular moments in history. In chapter one, I draw on Hall *et al*'s (1978) analysis of a major moral panic in the 1970s around mugging to make sense of the mobilisation of race by the new right and subsequent governments in times of economic and political crisis.

Education

Education and schooling are central to an analysis of Muslim youth as new folk devils today. Schools are places where relations of power and dominant cultural definitions are mediated and young people nego-tiate and contest issues of belonging, citizenship and identity. It is also in young people's local contexts that the minutiae of difference is worked out. Schools, colleges and universities, along with mosques, airports, bookshops and prisons, have come to be identified as spaces and places (Spalek, 2007) that may give rise to terror. Teachers, lec-turers, pastoral coordinators and other education and youth staff have been required, through counter-terror measures, to monitor students for signs of extremism. Staff have reportedly been asked to look for signs of extremism in children as young as four (Kundnani, 2009). Schools are declared guilty of allowing violent Muslim and Asian gangs to go un-challenged (see, for example, Bracchi, 2009). As well as mediating dominant relations of power, schools are sites of agency and resistance, individually and collectively expressed in ways that range from class-room resistance, playground and corridor talk to organised protests against imperialism (Cunningham and Lavallette, 2004).

This book is primarily about the ways in which Muslim boys make sense of their local environments at a time of significant economic, political and social change. The empirical study was constructed after the US and British coalition had declared a 'war on terror' following the terrorist attacks in New York in 2001. I am particularly interested in the resources that the boys draw on at a time when, we are told, old bonds of tradition and class have given way to individualisation. Theories of reflexive modernity (Giddens, 1991; Beck, 1992) posit an increasing trend towards individualisation as a result of the neo-liberalisation of labour markets, the decline of heavy industry and the growing casua-lisation of work. The old bonds of tradition, class and neighbourhood are said to have given way to increasingly individualised choices and life trajectories. On the other hand, dominant political and policy dis-courses continue to construct Pakistani and Bangladeshi families as culturally fixed and tradition bound.

The book sets out to challenge dominant representations of Muslim boys and young men as social problems, as modern day folk devils, by researching the ordinary lived experiences of 24 boys in a West Mid-lands town. I report on my qualitative research with boys aged 12-18 to explore a range of themes, issues and factors that shape the boys' orientation to schooling and their relationships in and out of school. The fieldwork was completed between May 2002 and October 2003 and it was clear that the wars in Afghanistan and Iraq were a significant backdrop to the boys' experiences of schooling, family, neighbourhood and locality and so was the declining manufacturing base which had precipitated widespread unemployment and racism in the areas they live in. All these factors influence the boys' take-up of various strategies and resources to counter and re-work, resist and sometimes reproduce dominant narratives of Muslim Asian boys as newly dangerous. The various identity strategies the boys employ indicate agency and creati-vity, but this agency needs to be read in the context of their structural constraints, which include their economic location in some of the most deprived neighbourhoods in England, as well as the powerful hege-monic cultural representations of them as social problems.

Muslims in Britain

The Muslim community in Britain is currently estimated to be between 1.8 million (Open Society Institute, 2002) and 2.4 million (Kerbaj, *Independent*, 2009) when account is taken of the younger age profile of Muslims and recent conversions to Islam in the aftermath of 9/11.

Ansari (2004) points out that there has been a significant Muslim pre-sence in Britain since the beginning of the nineteenth century. This included seamen and traders from the Middle East and students from the British Raj. However, most Muslim communities are the result of economic migration in the 1960s and 1970s, when large numbers of Indians, Pakistanis and later on Bangladeshis came to Britain in response to calls to help rebuild the economy in the aftermath of the Second World War. Since the 1970s, a steady flow of Muslim migrants have settled in Britain. These include Arabs and Turks in the 1970s and 1980s and, since the 1990s, eastern European, African and Middle Eastern Muslim refugees, who came from countries such as Nigeria, Bosnia and Kosovo, but also Afghanistan, Somalia and Iraq.

Roughly half the Muslim population of Britain lives in London. Others have settled mainly in the industrial Midlands, the northern mill towns and the West Coast of Scotland (Open Society Institute, 2002). The majority of Pakistani and Bangladeshi immigrants arriving in the UK in the 1960s and 1970s were land labourers and therefore classed as unskilled workers. By contrast, Indians were more likely to be members of the skilled working class or professional and business classes (Bagley, 1969 cited in Taylor, 1985). Large numbers of doctors, engineers, scientists and teachers arrived in Britain carrying vouchers for the 'special skills' category of the 1962 Immigration Act. In 1965-7, some 2,942 teachers from India and 577 from Pakistan were admitted (Rose *et al*, 1969). Also recruited were professional and business people from Kenya and Uganda in East Africa, many of whom fled programmes of Africanisation. Because they were primarily motivated by the need to find work, they tended to settle in inner cities where employment and housing were more readily available. They found work predominantly in manufacturing industries (Taylor, 1985) in urban areas (*ibid*; Garland, 1996) that have suffered most severely from the economic recession in England.

By most economic measures, however, Muslims, especially Pakistani and Bangladeshi communities, are the poorest and most disadvantaged of the ethnic minority communities living in England. For example, Pakistani men are twice as likely and Bangladeshi men three times more likely to be unemployed than white men. Pakistani and Bangladeshi women are four times more likely than white women to be jobless (ONS, 2006). Seventy per cent of Bangladeshi pupils and 60 per cent of Pakistani pupils live in the 20 per cent most deprived postcode areas (DfES, 2009).

Structure

Chapter one considers current public and policy concerns that position Muslim boys as social problems and locates these in a historical context. It pays particular attention to the ways in which race has been mobilised to justify coercive state measures in moments of economic and political crisis. Chapter two outlines the key concepts and positions that inform the book and sets the context for the empirical study. Chapters three to seven explore the main themes which emerged from the empirical study, focusing on politics and religion and identities (chapter 3), the construction of racialised hegemonic masculinities in school (chapter 4), and struggles over territory and turf, and over girls (chapter 5). Chapter six explores themes of race, nation and culture through analysis of the boys' sporting and musical affiliations and preferences, and chapter seven explores their educational and occupational aspirations. The final chapter reviews the main themes and explores some final implications of the research for education.

1

From the numbers game to terrorist suspects

Introduction

This chapter locates current concerns impacting on Muslim boys' schooling in a historical and policy context. I argue that since the 1960s, Muslim communities have consistently been characterised as policy problems in Britain and, through the discourse of cultural racism, as threatening to a mythic 'British way of life'. Initially, in the 1960s, this was as 'black' migrant workers in competition for jobs and services. But since the 1970s, problematic notions of 'cultural deficit' and 'culture clash' have been applied to read the children of migrant workers and most recently British-born minority youth as social problems.

The chapter is organised in three main sections. The first focuses briefly on how ethnic minorities have been conceptualised as a problem within British policy and public discourse. The focus of these concerns has shifted from 'race' in the 1960s, to ethnicity in the 1970s and 1980s and more recently to religion in the 1990s (Peach, 2005).

The second section looks at three interconnected and overlapping public and policy concerns that have served to position Pakistani and Bangladeshi communities as particularly problematic, and Muslim boys and young men in particular, as a new 'social time bomb' (Solomos and Back, 1994). Since 2001, these concerns have been fused together into a hegemonic cultural narrative of a violent and extremist underclass that is responsible for its own marginality. The third examines

1

recent policy responses through themes of race, nation and citizenship in state discourses since the late 1990s, particularly on education, in the context of a broader analysis of state polices for managing ethnic diversity and the impact of the 'war on terror'.

The numbers game
Racialising immigration

Like other black commonwealth immigrants arriving in Britain to help re-build the economy after the Second World War, Pakistani and Bangladeshi immigrants initially received a warm welcome. But they were soon treated with suspicion and hostility, particularly in the workplace, as competition for jobs grew. Throughout the period from 1948 to the 1960s, public and private debates focused on the extent of black immigration and its supposed impact on housing, the welfare state, crime and social problems.

The immigration issue was racialised by the specific focus on black migrants, who were openly described as 'undesirable' and a threat to a mythic 'British way of life'. They were alleged to import social problems such as prostitution and drug related crime, particularly the African-Caribbeans (Anwar, 1986; Layton-Henry, 1992; Solomos, 1992). These themes were evident in the aftermath of the Notting Hill and Nottingham riots in August and September, 1958. Although it was white youths who attacked blacks, media debates focused on the dangers of unrestricted immigration on the British nation, pushing the blame onto the black communities.

The resentment directed at immigrants coalesced into three main charges: they were alleged 'to do no work and to collect a rich sum from the Assistance Board' and to find housing when white residents could not. And they were charged with 'all kinds of misbehaviour especially sexual' (*The Times*, 3 September 1958 cited in Solomos, 1992). On the 27 August 1958, *The Times* had sought to explain the attacks on black people by whites as due to alleged misbehaviour, especially sexual and 'also sexual jealousy – the sight of coloured men walking along with white women'. The sexual theme was also stressed in the *Guardian* of 9 September 1958, in an article which reinforced the stereotype of black man as 'pimp'.

The huge publicity about the disturbances in Notting Hill and Nottingham put black immigration on the national agenda. Public opinion polls taken in their wake indicated widespread support for immigration controls. The racialisation was achieved in a coded way such that 'race' was not always mentioned but 'immigrant' was used as synonymous with 'black', which in turn became equated with 'problem'. The misuse of language became so prevalent that British-born blacks continued to be perceived as immigrants (Layton-Henry, 1992) and a whole range of anti-immigration activity developed from the mid-1950s. During and after the riots, extreme right wing groups focused their propaganda on the same issues and this sparked more racist attacks on black people.

Moral panics and the re-racialisation of the youth question

Concerns about race and immigration did not just spontaneously emerge in public debates. As Solomos (1992) has argued, the state played a central role in defining both the form and the content of policies and wider political agendas. The immigration issue focused heavily on race in the 1960s, and in the discourse on youth, race concerns were secondary to the problem of youth. But from the mid-1970s, as the Thatcher government prepared to take office, a new racialised discourse was constructed which positioned black African-Caribbean youth as the 'enemy within'.

Hall *et al*'s classic study, *Policing the Crisis* (1978), offers even thirty years on, a powerful analysis of how a new un-British phenomenon of mugging (violent street crime) was central to the new right's mobilisation of race as part of its attempt to manufacture consent for a new coercive state. It was a response to the economic crisis in the 1970s that signalled the end of the post Second World War social democratic state and the liberal consensus.

Immediately after the Second World War, Britain enjoyed a period of social democratic rule by both Labour and Conservative governments (1945-60). Internationally, this was the most sustained period of economic growth. In Britain, the Labour government of 1945-51 laid the foundations for the post-war consensus by establishing the welfare state, adapting capitalism and the labour movement to the mixed economy and committing itself to the free enterprise side of the Cold War. The Conservative government continued this trend, becoming

3

more interventionist in order to achieve economic expansion. By distri-
buting shares and bringing certain industries under state control, it
claimed to have a 'national property-owning democracy' (Prime
Minister Anthony Eden). The political realisation of the post-war consensus came with three consecutive Conservative victories, culminat-
ing in Macmillan's 'never had it so good speeches' in 1959 (Hall *et al*,
1978).

However, the consensus was economically unstable and as inflation rose
in the 1960s and ate into real wages, Britain fell behind her competitors.
A society deeply divided by class characterised Britain as poverty was
'rediscovered'. The 1960s saw the arrival of new social movements that
challenged the ideological consensus. Youth subcultural movements,
feminism, black power and the general middle class counter-culture
signified a crisis in the post war liberal consensus.

Drawing on a Gramscian analysis, Hall *et al* (1978) argued that the end
of the post-war liberal consensus created space for a new form of
political leadership but one that required a more coercive form of state
to manage the crisis caused by the decline in Britain's manufacturing
base. The Thatcher government took up that space, creating consent for
its neoliberal post welfarist policies through the use of moral panics
around race, youth and crime. Hall *et al* defined moral panic as an
'ideological displacement', 'a discrepancy between threat and reaction,
between what is perceived and what the perception is' (p29):

> A moral panic is one of the principal forms of ideological consciousness by
> means of which a silent majority is won over to the support of the increas-
> ingly coercive measure on the part of the state and lends its legitimacy to a
> more than usual exercise of social control. (Hall *et al*, 1978:221)

The media plays a crucial role in creating moral panics around particular events, as do its primary definers. Primary definers – key public
figures, politicians, and police with whom the media has a reciprocal
relationship – all rely on and are relied on by the media to provide information, which has an agenda-setting function. Further, Hall *et al* suggest that these relatively independent agencies do not simply respond
to moral panics; they often form part of the circle out of which moral
panics develop. 'It is part of the paradox [that] they advertently and

inadvertently amplify the deviancy they seem so absolutely committed to controlling' (*ibid*:52).

Until the 1960s, race concerns were secondary to the problem of youth. White working class young people were the main focus of adult anxieties and fears about new cultural styles. However, by the end of the 1960s, race was placed firmly on the political agenda. A renewal of the moral panic around race followed MP Enoch Powell's speeches of 1968, in which he identified immigration and race as a conspiracy against the silent majority. Relations between police and black communities, especially the African-Caribbean community, deteriorated. African-Caribbean boys and men, in particular, were identified as a threat to social order and police requested a tightening of laws which allowed them to stop and search black people. Terrorism and trade union power were identified as 'holding the nation to ransom' (Hall *et al*, 1978). The moral panic around mugging brought to centre stage, black African-Caribbean youth, who were constructed as lazy, resentful and who invoked the 'genuine fears' of white people that their nation was under threat.

By the mid-1980s, African-Caribbean youth were being characterised as a 'social time bomb' (Solomos and Back, 1996). The transformation of inner-city areas in relation to economic and social structures provided possibilities for the racialisation of such issues as employment, housing, education and the law. This racialisation process moved the focus of debate on from immigration itself to the identification of social 'problems' linked to race, particularly in relation to young African-Caribbeans in education, the police and urban policy (CCCS, 1982).

The idea that black youth were a 'social time bomb' (Solomos and Back, 1996) was reinforced by the inner-city disturbances in Brixton, Handsworth and Liverpool in 1981 and 1985. These were interpreted in the press, and by former MP Powell, as intimately linked to the size and concentration of the black population in certain areas. African-Caribbean youth were the main focus of such arguments, and culturalist explanations for the riots became institutionalised in state policies of multiculturalism that I discuss later in this chapter. The government commissioned the Scarman (Scarman, 1982) enquiry into the 'riots', which officially denied the existence of institutional racism in Britain and argued that a few individual police officers were racist but not the whole force. The discourses used by Scarman and the media painted a picture of community cultural breakdown and a 'cycle of pathological and deviant black culture' (Gilroy, 1987). The 'criminality' of the rioter was attributed to family breakdown, notably the absence of a father figure as a significant role model. Girls were prone to teenage pregnancy while boys drifted into illicit and criminal activities including drugs and street crime. The official policy response to the disturbances was to institutionalise multiculturalism – significantly, seen at the time as a solution to rioting not, as in the 2001 disturbances, the cause of it (Alexander, 2004).

New folk devils

Despite being actively involved in organised campaigns against racism and fascism (Sivanandan, 1989; Ramamurthy, 2006; Shain, 2009), Asian youth were publically stereotyped as passive, hardworking and obedient because of cultural deficit models that positioned Asian cultures as 'strong' and African Caribbean cultures as 'weak'.

By the late 1980s, the British discourse on minorities was shifting from ethnicity towards religion and, with it, the perception of Muslim Asian youth shifted from passive, hardworking and studious to volatile, aggressive and dangerous. This re-racialisation of working class youth as a 'problem' needs to be read in the context of the wider 'religious turn' which emerged in the space created by the end of Cold War politics and the demise of the former Soviet Eastern bloc in 1991. In England, the Rushdie affair was a major catalyst in the politicisation of Muslim identities. Groups previously identifying as Pakistani, Mirpuri or Bangladeshi were now defined and defined themselves as Muslims (Saghal and Yuval-Davis, 1992).

The controversy began in 1988 with the publication of a novel, *The Satanic Verses*, in which Salman Rushdie explored themes of cultural alienation, racism and the role of religion. Rushdie cast doubts on the authenticity of the Quran, implying that parts of it were the work of the devil. It was in England, and particularly in Bradford, that the reaction to the book was strongest. The first book burning was held in Bolton in December 1988, when 7,000 people staged a demonstration, but the greatest condemnation was directed at the widely publicised book burning in Bradford in January 1989. On 14 February 1989, the issuing of a fatwa on Rushdie provoked demonstrations against the book and led to scenes of anger, violence and destruction in many parts of the world. But it was the actions of young Asian men in Bradford that grabbed the attention of observers and social analysts.

Closely followed by the 1991 Gulf War, the fatwa placed in the spotlight Muslim communities and their practices. Media discussions focused mainly on religious dogmatism and on the implications of the controversy for British multiculturalism. The Rushdie affair served as a pivot for public and political debates about preserving a (white) British way of life, protecting western values of freedom and liberalism against alien, un-civilised, uncultured, and misogynistic Muslims, reviving colonial ideas of the backwardness and barbarity of Muslims and re-fuelling debates about the threat posed by unrestricted immigration to the British nation.

The Gulf War in 1991, the Bradford riots in 1995, the 2001 summer disturbances, 9/11, the London bombings in 2005 and numerous failed bomb plots have all continued to fuel fears about extremist Muslims, and the discourse conflates political events with the issue of violent Asian and Muslim gangs.

Current concerns

In the 1970s, older Asian men were portrayed as violent patriarchs, the perpetrators of honour crimes and the cause of runaway brides from forced marriages. Since the 1990s, young Muslim and Asian men have increasingly been redrawn in public discourses as violent and patriarchal. Stories about Muslim gangs raping, pimping and assaulting white girls make frequent tabloid headlines. In Germany in 2010, for example, the ex-central bank official and former finance senator, Thilo Sarrazin revived the arguments about an 'underclass' of poor immigrants and suggested that Islam produces violent young people. Sarrazin refers primarily to Turks in Germany but his argument explicitly stresses the 'Muslimness' of migrants in various nations including Britain, France, Norway and Holland, which, he suggests produces undereducated, over populated, overly fertile, largely unemployed communities that are also more prone to crime.

Sarrazin claims that tensions exist between traditional Muslim codes of honour, which apparently promote aggressive masculinity, and Muslim boys' underachievement compared with Muslim girls'. According to Sarrazin:

> frustration at school combines with sexual frustrations, both contributing to a build-up of aggression in the young men – for religious reasons, however, young girls are not sexually available before marriage. Even harmless sexual gestures are ruled out. Inappropriate role model, low-level educational achievement and sexual frustration can lead to an increased readiness to commit acts of violence, principally exercised in youth gangs that are the de facto homes of many Muslim immigrants.

As Kreikenbaum (2010) notes, these arguments are strongly reminiscent of underclass theories such as that proposed by Murray and Hernstein (1994), who purport to show African Americans to be intellectually less able and consequently economically poorer than American whites, and therefore more likely to be unemployed and involved in crime. Sarrazin proposes remedying the alleged problems of Muslim immigrants by means of forced labour and abolishing further immigration, and advocates ID cards for immigrants and a return to rote learning. These arguments and solutions resonate strongly with British government debates about the failings of multiculturalism. Muslims across Europe have been targeted as scapegoats for the declining economic status of European nation states when the manufacturing base has shifted to the east, notably to India and China. Attacks on Muslims through discourses of multiculturalism and integration are also employed by the state in attempts to justify drastically scaling back public and welfare state services (Zizek, 2010).

Similar views about the violent masculinity of Muslim young men were advanced in England by former Labour MP Ann Cryer. In 2003, she spoke out over claims of sexual abuse in her constituency of Keighley. Like Sarrazin, Cryer maintained that the problem needed to be seen in cultural and racial terms, saying, 'I am merely pointing out that all the victims of these terrible crimes are white girls and all the alleged perpetrators are Asian men'. She suggested that young Asian men in traditional communities were unable to pursue casual relationships like their white peers because they were tied to arranged marriages, and that because Asian communities were so restricted by cultural expectations around arranged marriage, Pakistani and Bangladeshi boys were targeting vulnerable white girls.

Former Home Secretary Jack Straw re-ignited the debate in January 2011, when he repeated Cryer's and Sarrazin's claims after nine men were convicted in Derby of sexual offences against white girls. He remarked that some Pakistani men saw white girls as 'easy meat' and the problem was specific to Pakistani heritage men who, 'fizzing and popping with testosterone' 'groomed' white girls because 'Pakistani-heritage girls are off-limits and because they are expected to marry Pakistani girls from Pakistan' (Straw, 2011).

Blaming a community's culture as these three commentators do deflects attention from the universally patriarchal underpinnings of sexual crimes and places the blame for violence on Islamic cultural practices. All conflate educational underachievement, criminality and the Islamification of Europe through the notion of a Muslim underclass. These three issues form a dominant cultural narrative of a Muslim underclass that is responsible for its own marginality. Each is discussed below.

1. 'Underachievement' in education and the labour market

Since the mid-1990s, male underachievement and concerns that girls outperform boys in education and the labour market have been a central preoccupation of policy makers across Britain, Australia and Canada. Despite feminist challenges to the reading of the statistical data (Skelton and Francis, 2005; Epstein *et al*, 1998) the discourse has positioned girls as achievers at the expense of boys, causing a feminist backlash. The backdrop for this apparent crisis in masculinity has been the economic restructuring in response to the decline in manufacturing and heavy industries and the consequent rise in a feminised service sector and large scale unemployment. For boys and men, these shifts have ended the old certainties associated with the transition from education to work and with it the guaranteed availability of a male bread-winner role.

While statistics on achievement (DfES, 2007a) show them to be among the losers in the achievement game, Pakistani and Bangladeshi boys have not been the focus of the concerns about boys' underachievement in general. As Archer argues (2003:23):

> Whereas problems of white masculinity have been located in terms of external factors e.g. changing environment conditions, the rise of feminism and improving girls' attainment, the problems associated with minority ethnic young men have been framed in terms of their 'race' and culture.

For example, following the 2001 disturbances in the northern towns, official explanations shifted attention away from the widespread disadvantage suffered by those communities, suggesting that 'expectations are ... very low in some areas and some occupations seem to be outside the knowledge and aspirations of some cultures' (Cantle, 2002:44). These arguments resonate strongly with the framework of cultural deficit employed in the 1970s, when the apparent underachievement of Asian children was explained by their lack of language and acculturation, rather than material disadvantage.

Where disadvantage is recognised, it serves to inform arguments about a Muslim underclass. Pakistanis and Bangladeshis emerged in the public imagination as an underclass when it was discovered that statistics on achievement up until the 1990s had masked Indian 'success' and Pakistani and Bangladeshi 'failure'. Separating out various subgroups comprising the South Asian category in the Youth Cohort Study in 1992 revealed a more differentiated picture. This showed Indians, more of whom are middle class, to be performing at least as well as white children, while Pakistani and Bangladeshi children achieved poorly. The Policy Studies Institute (1993) noted the disparity between Indians, who had better qualifications and job prospects, and Pakistani and Bangladeshis, who significantly lagged behind them. It was with the sensationalist reporting of these findings in a BBC Panorama documentary *Underclass in Purdah,* which aired in May 1993, that direct links were made for the first time between low Pakistani and Bangladeshi achievement, and employment and criminality. With gendered representations of boys as potential drug dealers, violent criminals and pimps, and Asian girls as passive victims of domestic and sexual violence and as prostitutes, *Underclass in Purdah* depicted young Muslims of Pakistani and Bangladeshi origin not only as a new underclass but also as a time bomb waiting to go off. Following hot on the heels of the Rushdie affair, the Gulf War in 1991, and an alleged scandal in 1992 about 'cheating' Pakistani cricketers, the documentary helped to cement the newly formed construction of Muslim Asian boys as a social problem.

As Gillborn (2008:59-60) has argued, recent statistics on ethnicity and achievement show a complex picture with girls performing better than boys across the board. Since 1992, the achievements of Pakistani and Bangladeshi young people have varied considerably, showing that existing inequalities are not fixed. All groups have enjoyed some improvement over the period but the black/white gap is almost as great as ever and both Bangladeshi and Pakistani students have experienced a period of growing inequality (*ibid*:60). There are few detailed trends for other Muslim minorities but recent research on Turkish youth (Enneli *et al*, 2005) and the Department for Communities and Local Government (DCLG, 2009a) show that Turkish Cypriots perform better academically than students from mainland Turkey, whose educational performance is similar to that of Pakistanis and Bangladeshis.

While they may be losing out at school, there is also evidence that Muslim students are more likely than their white working class peers to go to university. Modood (2006) argues, however, that because of socio economic disadvantage and radicalised institutional filtering, they are more likely to attend newer universities or as part-time students – which immediately rules out the most prestigious careers. Such statistics are also cited in media panics about the white working class losing out to ethnic minorities (eg Daley, 2008). This pitting against each other of different sections of the working class not only minimises the racial disadvantage suffered by black students but also reinforces a process whereby class becomes ethnicised. As Bottero (2009:7) argues:

> By presenting the white working class in ethnic terms, as yet another cultural minority in a (dysfunctional') 'multicultural Britain', commentators risk giving a cultural reading of inequality, focusing on the distinctive cultural values of disadvantaged groups, rather than looking at the bigger picture of how systematic inequality generates disadvantage. ... By stressing the whiteness of the white working class, the class inequality of other ethnic groups disappears from view. This sidesteps the real issue of class inequality, focusing on how disadvantaged groups compete for scarce resources rather than exploring how that scarcity is shaped in the first place.

2. Violent criminality, gangs and riots

Recent representations of Muslim young men as rapists echo similar stories across western nation states, such as the accusation of gang rapes by Lebanese youth in Australia that sparked the Cronulla 'riots' in 2005 (Poynting, 2006). North African youth in France were branded as rapists around the time of the Paris Banlieues 'riots' (Cesari, 2006), and in England an unconfirmed charge of rape was widely seen as the main trigger for the Lozells disturbances in Birmingham in 2005 when clashes between Asian and African-Caribbean youth led to the violent death of bystander Isaiah Young-Sam. These images of brutal sexuality are highly potent because they resonate strongly with the images of hyper-sexualised African men discussed in relation to the coverage of the Notting Hill disturbances; they also draw on colonial fears about the barbarity and brutality of Arab and Muslim men, particularly in their targeting of pure white women (Fryer, 1988; Ware, 1992). The focus on violent masculinity often centres specifically on Muslim gangs. The events leading up to the 2001 disturbances in northern towns were central to a media construction of the Asian Gang (Alexander, 2000).

The riots in 2001 and the Asian gang

Between April and July 2001, clashes involving whites, South Asians and the police broke out across Oldham, Burnley and Bradford, and later Stoke-on-Trent, leading to 395 arrests and an estimated £12 million in damage to property. Over 450 people were injured in disturbances in-volving 1400 people (Denham, 2002). The disturbances in Oldham, where the police in riot-gear battled with over 500 men for control of the streets in the mainly Asian area of Glodwick for three nights in late May, were described as the 'worst riots in Britain for 15 years' (Carter, 2001). The false accusation that Asian gangs had created no-go areas for whites in Oldham cast them as the perpetrators of crime rather than victims of racism and racial harassment was recorded as a significant factor in the disturbances (Kalra, 2002; Bagguley and Hussain, 2008; Rhodes, 2009).

Various explanations were offered in policy and public debates im-mediately following the events. Many of these explanations pointed to racism, deprivation and high unemployment in the northern towns and cities. However, as Alexander (2004) has argued, the media reporting centred around two dominant explanations – a culturalist reading dwelling on the pathology of Asian cultures and a structuralist argu-ment centring on material factors such as poverty and socioeconomic disadvantage. Both are found in the following excerpt from the *Observer* (22 April, 2001):

> Isolated in downtrodden towns where work is scarce, they [Asian communities] are finding life increasingly difficult. Drugs have entered their communities, violent gangs have followed and racism is never far away. They are becoming ghettos. Fears that estates in Bradford and Oldham may become virtual no-go areas for other races, especially whites, could yet become a reality ... In the tight-knit community like Lidget Green everyone knows who to contact to score a hit. It is virtually impossible for an outsider to break in.

Like much of the media reporting of the events, the article refers to a dominant stereotype of Asian gangs involved in drug crimes. This article, as Alexander notes, fuses notions of cultural (ethnic/racial) dysfunction (ghettos and no-go areas, insiders/outsiders) through accounts of no-go areas, presenting images of social breakdown (drugs gangs and violence). The article makes reference to the Ousely Report on Bradford, repeating the warning of 'the growing threat of self-segregation' by the city's diverse ethnic communities (Ousley, 2001), and reproducing the notion of cultural difference in relation to Muslim communities.

As a number of commentators (Kalra, 2002; Bagguley and Hussain, 2008; Rhodes, 2009) have noted, the electoral wards in which the disturbances took place were some of the poorest in the country. All were ranked amongst the 20 per cent most deprived in the country and parts of Oldham and Burnley were in the top one per cent. Incomes in each area were also among the lowest in the country (Denham, 2002). In some of the wards, it was reported that unemployment rates among Asian men were as a high as 50 per cent (Amin, 2002). All the towns had suffered acutely from the de-industrialisation of their economies and now exhibited high levels of residential segregation and unemployment. Bradford, Oldham and Burnley all had majority white populations (Bagguley and Hussain, 2008). There was significant evidence of far-right activity and racist attacks on Asian people in Oldham and Burnley, a major factor in precipitating the disturbances.

However, the official reports framed the riots through a discourse of 'parallel lives', as in: 'separate educational arrangements, community and voluntary bodies, employment, places of worship, language, social and cultural networks, means that many communities operate on the basis of a series of parallel lives' (Cantle, 2001:9). It was argued that this parallel living had led to widespread ignorance of 'others'. The Cantle report characterised racism as the 'natural' result of ignorance or lack of knowledge about others.

> There is little wonder that ignorance about each others' communities can easily grow into fear; especially where this is exploited by extremist groups determined to undermine community harmony and foster division. (2001: 9)

Not only did the press coverage and official reports take little account of racism, they also rejected its significance in shaping the socioeconomic locations of the 'rioters'. They ignored the way that Asian males had been demonised and criminalised as a defiant group prone to violence and criminality (Alexander, 2004; Bagguley and Hussain, 2008; Rhodes, 2009).

The emphasis on self-segregation shifted attention away from the wide range of material and social factors that might lead to Asian communities being segregated – such as racism in housing markets, the racism of landlords, council housing policies, the propensity for racist attacks, and the fact that Asians are often priced out of the market. Rhodes (2009) argues that the naturalisation of inequalities within the official responses to the riots relied on and reproduced a form of cultural racism which cast South Asians as the Others, with cultural practices and traits deemed to threaten social cohesion. The reactions echoed the themes in the reports of the 1980s' disturbances (Benyon and Solomos, 1987; Gilroy, 1987).

Young Muslim Asian males were cast as criminals much more forcefully than their white counterparts. The dominant representations of the rioters as young Asian males between the ages of 17 and 30 are open to challenge (see Bagguley and Hussain, 2008:50). Figures from Burnley, for example, reveal that 27 per cent of those arrested were whites over the age of 30, and only 9 per cent of those arrested were South Asians aged between 17 and 20. The media reports and political commentaries created a picture of Asian male criminality and 'out of control' gangs. One consequence was the tougher sentences given to the Asian men, who were charged for up to five years (Alexander, 2004; Bagguley and Hussain, 2008). The Labour Home Secretary was keen to view the riots in terms of criminality (Alexander, 2004) through the lens of intergenerational 'schizophrenia', thus repeating familiar themes of culture clash. He suggested that Muslim Asians were torn between the culture and authority of their parents and their identities as British citizens and rejected both. The riots were therefore viewed as a rejection of Britishness rather than a call to be treated as equal citizens (Kundnani, 2001; Amin, 2002).

3. Terrorists, radicals and extremists

The Rushdie affair was a major turning point for British Muslims, not only in terms of the re-categorisation of various ethnic (Mirpuri, Bangladeshi, Pakistani) groups into religious (Muslim) ones that it invoked, but also because it occurred around the same time as other protests involving Muslim youth in Europe's inner cities. For example, when three schoolgirls in France were sent home from school for wearing the *hijab* in 1989, it sparked a major controversy about the relationship between Islam and the secular values institutionalised in French democracy.

Arising in the context of changing economic and political social circumstances and the rise of political Islam globally, protests and mobilisations involving Muslims became increasingly marked by a dominant focus on religion. Such protests have since been read as signalling the emerging radicalisation of Muslim youth across Europe and beyond, representing a generalised threat to western democratic ideals. Over the last decade but especially since the London transport bombings in July 2005, policy and political analysts have been concerned with trying to understand why young Muslims may be turning towards more radical versions of Islam. Such explanations have emphasised:

- the alienation of Muslim youth from the processes of local democracy (Cantle, 2001; Denham, 2002)
- their alienation from elders within their communities: intergenerational conflict
- the role of information and communications technology and especially the internet as a possible source of radicalisation (Cornish, 2008)
- frustration at western foreign policy, especially Britain and the US, in the Middle East and Afghanistan (Choudhury, 2007)
- the personal and social circumstances encountered by those who were alleged to have engaged in terrorist activities, that they are 'born on the wrong side of the tracks'[1] (Abbas, 2005).

Education is central to current discourses of radicalisation and extremism. In a paper reported to parliament by Tony Blair in the aftermath of the 2005 terrorist attacks, two main categories of 'at risk' Muslims were reported: those who had few qualifications and were underachievers, and university students who, because of blocked social mobility, might be vulnerable to the radical Islamist groups operating on university campuses (Leppard and Fielding, 2005). In an independent but contested and controversial report, Glees and Pope (2005) made a number of recommendations about countering the threat of extremism in educational institutions. One of these was reminiscent of the assimilationist bussing[2] policy in the 1960s: it suggested that to prevent radicalisation, universities control and limit the number of Muslims allowed to register for degree courses.

Some analysts suggest that it is impossible to identify a root cause of radicalisation. Others, however, such as Choudhury (2007) suggest a linear progression from feelings of discrimination and perceptions of blocked social mobility, to being preyed upon by members of radical organisations such as *Hizb'uTahrir* and the now disbanded *Al Muhajiroun,* who work on re-defining the and the individual's self-concept and perspective on society from a radical anti-western perspective. Converts are said to be the most vulnerable since they lack the relevant religious literacy to challenge the world view presented by these radical groups as being Islamic (*ibid*).

In a later section I consider recent government policy responses to the challenge of radicalisation and the extent to which government funding and research effort has been disproportionate to the threat. Less than a third of all such offences lead to convictions (Travis, 2009a). Applying the radicalisation thesis to young Muslims raises two further problems. First, there is a tendency to portray any assertion of Islamic identity as a sign of extremism and a rejection of British citizenship. Second, the radicalisation thesis denies agency to Muslim young people while at the same time as being a gendered discourse. Muslim boys and young men are constructed as politically disaffected and alienated and therefore at risk of being brainwashed into extremism. Muslim girls and women are assumed to be oppressed into wearing veils. As Bepplar Spahl (2010) notes, 'many [Muslim] girls wear the veil even though their mothers don't, that is, as a political statement'.

Shabina Begum, the Luton school girl who, in March 2005, won (and later lost) the right to wear the *jilbab* (a long loose gown that reveals only face and hands) to school, illustrates both these tendencies. Although Shabina appeared in public as highly articulate, confident and determined, asserting that the decision to fight for the right to wear such clothing was her own choice, the media pounced on the fact that her brother was a member of the radical Islamic group *Hiz-bu-Tahrir* and must therefore have put her up to it[3]. In much of the media coverage her brother was pictured lurking menacingly in the background, thus portraying Shabina as a puppet of the avowedly radical extremist group he represented. Controversy in England in 2006 over the *hijab* presented Muslim women who asserted their right to take up the veil as the bearers of a backward patriarchal Muslim culture that was 'refusing to integrate' (Werbner, 2007; Shain, 2010), shifting the blame for segregation and social problems identified in the Cantle (2001) and Ousley (2001) reports that followed the inner city disturbances in 2001 firmly onto the Muslim community itself.

A very British hero: Amir Khan and a positive representation of Muslim masculinity?

A seeming contrast to the negative portrayal of Muslim boys in public and policy space is to be found in media and political representations of Amir Khan. A second-generation British Pakistani Muslim from Bolton, he won the lightweight boxing silver medal at the Athens Olympics in 2004 at the age of 17. Within a year, he announced his intention to turn professional and was propelled to the status of a role model for British youth. Since then Khan has been championed by high profile figures, including politicians of all persuasions, as 'a credit to the country' and a 'wonderful role model' (Hazel Blears, former communities minister, cited in *Sky News*, 2008), a 'charming son of Islam' (2005, *Daily Mail*, 2005) and 'true Brit' (Parsons, 2008), someone 'who has the guts to say he's proud and British' (*Sun*, 2005).

Khan's first professional fight was against David Bailey on 16 July 2005 – just a week after the London transport bombings. His, albeit quiet, public condemnation of these events further strengthened his appeal as a 'moderate' Muslim. As Kundnani observed, '[since 2001] two distinct categories of Muslim rapidly emerged: the 'good' and the 'bad'; the 'moderates', 'liberals' and 'secularists' versus the 'fundamentalists', 'extremists' and 'Islamists'' (Kundnani, 2009:35). Khan's appeal lies not just in the fact that he is a 'moderate', but that he is a moderate who has the 'guts to say he's Muslim and proud'. Khan's status as a 'good' Muslim was supported when in 2008, former leader and founder of *Al Mohajiroun* Omar Bakri Mohammed labelled Khan an 'ignorant deviant' for wearing the British flag.

However, as Burdsey (2007) asserts, Khan's elevation to role model cannot be understood without reference to wider national policy discourses of segregation and extremism that currently shape the construction of hyper-masculinised and disaffected young Muslim males. It is only within the framework of segregation that Khan's ability to transcend racial and ethnic barriers can be read. Tony Parsons, for example, drew on a discourse of 'parallel lives' when he recalled 'watching him before a Ricky Hatton fight in Manchester, signing autographs all night long for big white geezers who had probably never spoken to a Muslim before' (Parsons, 2009). He is positive about Khan's ability to bring together 'segregated' and disparate communities. In doing so, Khan represents 'a true symbol of hope for this country', but only if he does not mention what Parsons calls the 'r' (racism) word'. When Khan did cite racism as a reason for not being nominated for British sports personality of the year in 2008, Parsons accused him of 'whining':

> So I hope he is not going to keep whining about how Britain doesn't respect him. We love you, Amir, and we have proved it. Your suggestion that America is a better bet for Muslims is laughable. Ever heard of a gaff called Guantanamo Bay? (Parsons, 2009)

The reference to Guantanamo is interesting, as it invokes notions of American brutality and intolerance at the same time as notions of British tolerance. As Rattansi (2004) argues, the discourse of British fairness and tolerance, to which this extract alludes, ignores long standing prejudice and violence against immigrants and newcomers. Racism, in other words, is as embedded in British culture as 'tolerance'.

I suggest that the role-modelling of Khan has been achieved via the folk-devilling of the majority of working class Muslim boys. I agree with Burdsey (2007) that Khan's elevation to national role model represents a particular political construction that reproduces contradictory representations of Muslim young men. Ultimately, it both relies on and re-inforces negative, homogenised and pathologised constructions of the vast majority of working class Muslim males. The celebration of Khan is achieved within a framework of citizenship aligned to neo-liberalism. Khan is a winner and a responsible citizen (despite a conviction in 2008 for dangerous driving) who is hardworking and above all an entre-preneur. Despite the violence of his sport he stands as an oppositional figure to the image of violent Muslim masculinity. For example, when Conservative leader David Cameron opened Khan's Gloves gym in Bolton in January 2008, he supported this dualistic and contradictory representation of Muslim masculinity:

> Some people might say 'it is not a good idea to get young people boxing' but it is so much better for people to come here, get fit, learn about boxing than hang around on street corners and look up to the drug dealers on their housing estates. Young people need to have role models like Amir Khan.

Cameron's comments need to be read in the context of the speech (to criticise former Prime Minister Gordon Brown's apparent abandon-ment of the 'respect' agenda) on youth violence he was preparing to deliver in Salford later the same day. He went there to argue that Britain was creeping into a social acceptance of violence, accusing the New Labour government of staggering complacency on the issue. He called for tougher powers for magistrates, more prison places, and an abandonment of the bureaucracy surrounding police monitoring and recording of crime. According to Cameron, society needed to be 're-socialised' in order to 're-claim our streets' from criminals who had turned them in no-go areas. He went on to to declare that:

> We're collapsing into an atomised society, stripped of the local bonds of association which help tie us together ... Aggression is feted. Verbal abuse celebrated. Contempt for others rewarded. ... We cannot go on like this. How many more parents have to bury their children, how many more neighbourhoods have to be torn asunder, how much more blood has to be spilt on our streets before we choose hope over fear, order over chaos, and community over division?

Cameron's comments plug into wider, historic panics about working class youth. Young people are represented as violent, out of control and lacking respect (Pearson, 1983; Cohen, 2002). However, Cameron also evokes the racialised imagery of drug-ridden neighbourhoods in which youth wander aimlessly and hang around with no ambition or drive. By contrast, Amir is depicted as a self-made entrepreneur – representing all the things associated with 'good' British citizenship. Cameron, along with others, implies that if only all Muslim youth were as aspirational and ambitious as Khan they would be able to 'work' their way out of these bleak neighbourhoods, avoid future unemployment and improve their life chances. Cameron's views invoke the culture of poverty thesis which links underachievement and poor life chances to community or parental attitudes.

As Burdsey (2007) notes, this trivialises or ignores the reasons why so many Muslim youth do not feel a great sense of pride in their British-ness – British foreign policy, the over policing of them through measures such as Stop and Search (which increased 302% between 2001 and 2003), and the criminalisation of them as a 'suspect' population when they do engage in legal political action. For example, disproportionately harsh sentences were issued in January 2010 to the Gaza protesters who demonstrated in December 2008 and January 2009. Twenty two custodial sentences were handed out to mainly young Muslim men between the ages of 17 and 30, for public order offences that included throwing a stone at a police shield. Most of the 119 arrested were young Muslim men (including Algerians, Palestinians and Pakistanis) and 78 of them were charged. Many of the arrests took place in dawn raids months after the events and some allegedly involved police brutality. It has also been reported that many of those arrested were very young, the youngest being a boy of 12, and many others were under 19, in full time education and had no criminal record. Many were on their first demonstration (Milne, 2010a)[4].

Policy frameworks: 'race', nation and citizenship

Since the 1960s, policies for the management of ethnic diversity have been based on complex ideologies that range from 'assimilation' (the expectation on immigrants to abandon their language and cultural norms and practices in favour of those of the host society) and 'integration' (acceptance of the majority culture's laws, customs and values through partial assimilation) to 'multiculturalism' (the recognition of a plurality of cultures) (Cheong *et al*, 2007). Grosvenor (1997) observed that: 'these identified shifts in policy are more apparent than real'. He argues that: 'they exist in the sphere of articulation rather than in practice' and that 'a clear, coherent consistent and uniform' policy goal is readily identifiable running through government circulars, advisory notes, select committee documents and political speeches during the period, which reveals 'an enduring commitment to assimilation' (1997: 49-50). Some commentators (Kundnani, 2001; Back *et al*, 2002) describe New Labour's strategy of community cohesion as a return to assimilationism – a major policy shift away from multiculturalism.

Grosvenor is correct to recognise assimilation as a policy goal, predating the Thatcher and Major governments; in Gilroy's (2004) view it could be said to reflect postcolonial melancholia or a harking back to the good old days of Empire. However, cohesion (race) policies since the late 1990s do represent a more concerted and strongly articulated response to the presence of minorities. Governmental and policy responses have been much more focused since then, supported by many reiterations about the concrete detail of unacceptable Otherness – such as forced marriages, the veil – and translated via an expanded state apparatus into policies for managing populations: citizenship classes and ceremonies, detention without trial and targeted policing and surveillance of 'suspect' (mainly Muslim, asylum seeker and foreign student) communities. The next section looks at recent policies that have implicated educational institutions in the surveillance, monitoring and containment of populations identified as 'problematic'.

One nation under New Labour

At the heart of all our work, however, is one central theme: national renewal. Britain re-built as one nation, in which each citizen is valued and has a stake; in which no-one is excluded from opportunity and the chance to develop their potential; in which we make it, once more, our national purpose to tackle social division and inequality. (Blair, 1997)

Race was, as we have seen, a central political symbol in the rise of the new right. It was 'mobilised to explain the demise of the post-war liberal consensus, economic decline, welfare dependency and a general lapse in social order and traditional moral value' (Ansell, 1997:26). The centrality of race and nation to the New Labour project reflects continuity with the previous Thatcherite project but whereas Thatcherism drew on a conception of Britain as divided between 'two nations', New Labour adopted a one-nation approach as part of its Third Way rhetoric. As Jessop (2003) has argued:

> Tory populism increasingly took the form of a unification of a privileged nation of 'good citizens' who were 'hard working', against a contained and subordinated nation which extended beyond the inner cities and their ethnic minorities to include much of the non-skilled working class outside the south East.

In Thatcher's construction of the 'British Nation' there was no room for 'welfare scroungers', the 'work-shy', the 'immoral' and trade unions who were depicted as by-products of post-welfarism coupled with a decline of moral values (Scraton, 1987).

By contrast, the Blairite 'Third Way' in public policy was based on the recognition that the neo-liberal reformulation of the social order needed a connecting and cohesive bond which New Labour set out to achieve via its construction of a single nation, united around 'community' and trust and supported by theories of social capital (Home Office, 2005). Blair consistently promoted the idea that Britain is composed of a 'single' nation in which opportunity can be shared by all. But at the same time, New Labour governments, especially from 2001, posed multiculturalism and ethnic identification as a threat to 'the nation' and, engaged in an ambitious project of redefining Britishness around notions of 'active citizenship', 'rights and responsibilities' and paid work (Worley, 2005).

This 'new' approach to managing diversity (Gilroy, 2004) positioned some groups, notably Muslims, asylum seekers and generally those not in paid employment as outside the nation and its interests. At the same time as promising equality for all, New Labour continued to promote the market as the way forward and achievement as the solution to social exclusion, especially through education policy. To date, the Coalition government has promoted privatisation of education as the solution to disadvantage and economic decline. Thus raced and classed inequalities continue to be marginalised in the interests of a relentless pursuit of success, achievement and global competitiveness, deepening existing inequalities and divisions.

Multiculturalism before New Labour

Although it emerged from below as a challenge to previous assimila-tionist polices for the management of immigration, multiculturalism was not officially adopted by the state until after Scarman published his report into the inner city disturbances of 1981. State institutionalised funding of separate ethnic groups produced not only a backlash from the right wing press but also from the left. Anti-racists (neo-Marxists) in particular claimed that the policy was a deliberate state attempt to weaken the solidarity that had been built across the left and the black community. From an anti-racist perspective, multiculturalism was always a double-edged sword (Kundnani, 2001). Initially, multicultura-lism represented a defensive survival strategy against New Right popular racism, but as political black communities became radicalised, mere survival was not enough. Multiculturalism changed from a line of defence to a mode of control:

> Multiculturalism now meant taking black culture off the streets – where it had been politicised and turned into a rebellion against the state – and putting it in the council chamber, in the classroom and on the television, where it could be institutionalised, managed and reified. Black culture was thus turned from a living movement into an object of passive contempla-tion, something to be 'celebrated' rather than acted on. Multiculturalism became an ideology of conservatism, of preserving the status quo intact, in the face of a real desire to move forward. (Kundnani, 2001)

While neo-Marxists held that polices were not designed to deliver race equality, defenders of multiculturalism argued that most multicultural policies were often abandoned before they had a chance to work or were mostly cosmetic and never adequately funded (Tomlinson, 2008). Both positions support Ball's observation that during the Thatcher and Major years, multiculturalism and anti-racism became subjected to a 'dis-course of derision' (Ball, 1990) and an explicitly 'colour-blind' approach to policy was pursued by the major government (Tomlinson, 2008).

New right critiques focused on multiculturalism as a 'looney left' obses-sion (Grosvenor, 1997), arguing that schools should promote British culture. The responsibility for transmitting minority cultures lay within the homes and the minority communities themselves. As Grosvenor (*ibid*:85) observed:

The Education Reform Act of 1988 can justifiably be described as representing a victory for the radical right in policy making. It was a victory achieved through the creation of a moral panic where everything connected with anti-racist education – LEAs teachers, advisers, curriculum projects – was presented as being ideologically unsound, culpable and at variance with British traditions and values. It was a victory in which the superior nature of the British 'way of life' was asserted over all other cultural variants.

Grosvenor asserted that the Education Reform Act was profoundly assimilationist. The legislation was based on a conception of the 'nation' as politically and culturally indivisible. As Baker stated in September 1987 when he introduced the conservative educational reform programme:

There is so much distraction, variety and uncertainty in the modern world that in our country today children are in danger of losing any sense at all of a common culture and a common heritage. The cohesive role of the national curriculum will provide our society with a greater sense of identity. (Kenneth Baker, cited in Grosvenor, 1997:86)

The 1992 White Paper and 1993 Education Act, *Choice and Diversity, a New Framework for Schools* argued that 'proper regard should continue to be paid to the national's Christian heritage and traditions'. In the context of wider polices of opting out, parental choice and competition between schools, racism in education became accepted under the new right as a market force (Gewirtz, 2001).

Institutional racism

Against this background the incoming New Labour government's decision to proceed with a public enquiry into the death of Stephen Lawrence seemed to mark a significant break with the Conservative approach to race. The publication of the Inquiry into Stephen Lawrence's murder seemed to support this new vision of a modern, multicultural Britain and the strengthening of existing race relations policy through the Race Relations (Amendment) Act 2000 and the Human Rights Act 1998 signalled New Labour's commitment to tackling race inequalities.

The Race Relations (Amendment) Act came into force in September 2002. It placed a new enforceable duty on public authorities of non-discrimination, as well as actively promoting racial equality. Educational institutions were legally required to prepare written policies on race equality; to assess the impact of their policies on ethnic minority pupils, staff and parents, with the emphasis on the attainment of ethnic minority pupils; and to monitor levels of attainment in relation to the school population.

Even in the first two years, however, it was clear that the legislation was not being taken seriously. The Commission for Racial Equality (CRE, 2003) noted that only handful of authorities were actually complying with the new Race Relations Amendment Act's requirements. The Ajegbo review (DfES, 2007) of *Diversity in the Curriculum* also supported this observation, arguing that 'issues of 'race' and diversity are not always high on schools' agendas (2007:34). Even before the end of New Labour's first term in office, combating institutional racism and promoting equal opportunities had arguably been watered down into an empty and meaningless concept of 'valuing diversity' which over-emphasised the 'celebration of differences' at the expense of tackling inequalities and material disadvantage (Mahony and Hextall, 2000). By 2003, the Home Secretary was able to state that the concept of institutional racism had 'missed the point' and that, 'It's not the structures created in the past, it's the processes to change structures in the future and it's individuals at all levels who do that' (Blunkett, 2003).

The shift to integration and cohesion

By New Labour's second term, institutional racism had virtually disappeared from the agenda and a new official race relations policy was underway. The Community Cohesion agenda emerged as a direct response to the civil disturbances that occurred in the northern towns in June 2001. But it was given further fuel after the 9/11 attacks were officially connected to Muslim extremists and the US and Britain officially declared a 'war on terror'.

The official reports (Cantle, 2001; Denham, 2002) into the causes of the riots identified the 'self-segregation' of Pakistani and Bangladeshi communities as the major problem. It was argued that whilst physical segregation was nothing new, the fact that white and Asian people's lives barely touched was cause for concern. Segregation prevented young people from actively participating in processes of local democracy, leaving them open to misinformation at best and potential radicalisation and 'extremism' at worst. In addition to citing language proficiency or the lack of it as a major factor in the cultural segregation of communities, Denham (2002) also called for an 'open, honest' debate about multiculturalism in Britain and a new strategy of community cohesion that would promote a greater sense of 'shared values and common citizenship to help bind Britain's diverse ethnic communities'.

Trevor Philips ignited a fierce debate about the issue when he suggested that Britain was 'sleepwalking into segregation' (Phillips, 2005). In terms of the policy reading of Muslim communities, what was once seen as 'good' social capital – the tightness of Asian family ties – was now being recast as 'bad'. In Robert Putnam's terms, Asian communities possessed too much 'bonding capital' and not enough 'bridging capital' (Cheong *et al*, 2007) – that is, they were constructed as too tightly knit and insufficiently outward facing; they needed to build on their social networks if they were to work their way out of marginalisation. As Burnett (2009) points out, community cohesion polices represent the soft end of coercive state strategies for managing such problem populations.

From 2001, British governments engaged in a project of redefining British citizenship around notions of cohesion and integration and, increasingly, 'British values'. For New Labour, this was largely conceptualised and pursued through its policies on immigration, namely the White Paper *Secure Borders Safe Haven* (Home Office, 2002) and Nationality, Immigration and Asylum legislation. Its 'managed migration' approach, as Flynn argues, has been:

> ... informed by a larger view of modernity and the meaning and potential of the processes of globalisation, the government is pushing for a system of managed migration which is based almost exclusively on utilitarian principles – in particular that the movement of people across the globe should be guided at every point by the economic objectives of growth and modernisation. From this standpoint, the old world of universal rights in the migration field exemplified by the right to asylum for those with a well-founded fear of persecution, is obsolete. In the new world of globalised reality, the concept of rights, if it is applicable at all, should be reserved for those who have made themselves useful to the needs of a growing and dynamic world economy, and who are actively contributing to its further development. (Flynn, 2003:5-6)

In this new managed migration strategy, economic migrants were welcome if there was need for them but political asylum continued to be constructed as 'bogus'. In *Secure Borders* David Blunkett justified a new robust system for managing migration with reference to the need for 'us' 'to be secure within our sense of belonging and identity':

> To enable integration to take place and to value the diversity it brings, we need to be secure within our sense of belonging and identity and therefore to be able to reach out and to embrace those who come to the UK ... Having a clear, workable and robust nationality and asylum system is the pre-requisite to building the security and trust that is needed. Without it, we cannot defeat those who would seek to stir up hate, intolerance and prejudice. (Home Office, 2002)

But the core of this Britishness, or what is really Englishness (Back *et al*, 2002), was never clearly defined. Sometimes it was the opposite of genital mutilation and forced marriages[5], at other times the 'British way' has referred to 'fair play and tolerance'[6]. In Gordon Brown's speeches (2006), 'hard work, effort and enterprise' were reframed as core British values, again betraying the New Labour's re-alignment of British citizenship with a neo-liberal state.

The 'war on terror' and 'suspect communities'

Since the end of the Cold War, there has been creeping concern over a new form of global enemy – international terrorism – that is inspired more by religious extremism and ethnic separatism than by politics or ideology. But it was not until after September 2001 that the US and Britain declared a full-scale 'war on terror' (Pantazis and Pemberton, 2009:650). The 'war on terror' has been central to the emergence of a new security discourse that positions Western liberal democracies as under threat by Islamic fanaticism, and Muslims as the new enemy within.

In Britain, the increasing scrutiny of Muslims began in the aftermath of the Rushdie affair in 1989, but concerns about the supposed radicalisation of Muslims spiralled after 2001. Following the July 2005 London bombings, Muslims have come to be identified as a new 'enemy within' (Kundnani, 2007). In earlier discourses of the 'war on terror', extremists were constructed in opposition to the vast majority of Muslims who were characterised as law abiding and peaceful. However, following the

London transport bombings, even before it had been established that the suicide bombers were British Muslims, Blair made an unambiguous link between the bombings and Muslims, saying, 'I welcome the statement put forward by the Muslim Council who know that those people did not act in the name of Islam' (Blair, 2005). These sentiments were echoed in counter-terrorism strategy which, since 2005, made direct links between terror and Islam.

> The principal current terrorist threat is from radicalised individuals who are using a distorted and unrepresentative version of Islam to justify violence. Such people are referred to in this paper as Islamist terrorists. They are however, a tiny minority within the Muslim communities here and abroad. Muslim communities themselves do not threaten our security; indeed they make a great contribution to our country. The Government is therefore working in partnership with Muslim communities to help them prevent extremists from gaining influence here. (Home Office, 2006)

After the 2005 bombings, Home Office Minister John Denham continued with the thrust of Blair's argument that only a minority of Muslims may be involved in terrorism. But this did not mean that the wider community was exempt from suspicion:

> Few terrorist movements have lasted long enough without a supportive community. A supportive community does not necessarily condone violence and certainly, most people in it would not want to become personally involved ... whether or not they condone violence, they see terrorists as sharing their worldview as part of the struggle to which they belong. (Denham cited in McGhee, 2008:69)

In February 2009, the Home Office spelled out who these people might be in the 'supportive community':

> ...it's about the stay-at-home mum, the taxi driver, the neighbour, the dinner lady ... the student – all of those whose decisions and actions contribute towards making an environment in which extremism can flourish or falter. (Blears, 2009)

What is significant about these constructions of a 'supportive community' is the way in which the *whole* Muslim community is implicated in terrorism. They are assumed to shield terrorists even though they may not be directly involved in terrorism. Such notions have been central to the new racist discourse that constructs Muslims as a 'suspect

community'. Adapting Hillyard's (1993) application of the term originally applied to the Irish community in the 1970s and 1980s, Pantazis
and Pemberton define a suspect community as:

> ... a sub-group of the population that is singled out for state attention as
> being 'problematic'. Specifically in terms of policing, individuals may be
> targeted, not necessarily as a result of suspected wrong doing, but simply
> because of their presumed membership of that sub-group. Race, ethnicity,
> religion, class, gender, language, accent, dress, political ideology or any
> combination of these factors may serve to delineate their group. (Pantazis
> and Pemberton, 2009:649)

The construction of Muslims as a suspect community also signals a pre-
emptive and increasingly coercive and punitive state approach to Muslim communities which is justified by a 'security' discourse. In July 2010
for example, security cameras were removed from two 'Muslim' areas of
Birmingham after pressure from residents. Forty four of these cameras
were hidden, fuelling the notion of British Muslim communities as sus-
picious – a racist discourse that can be traced to the colonial period
(Lawrence, 1982; Fryer, 1988). Perhaps the most contentious of recent
government strategies has been the Preventing Violent Extremism (PVE)
pathway that emerged out of the Labour government's Contest strategy
(Home Office, 2009). The educational implications of this strategy are
analysed next.

The 'war on terror' and education

As Jackson *et al* (2007) point out, the dominant discourses of global
security and the 'war on terror' have undoubtedly affected the broader
priorities of educational institutions, especially on the research culture
and practices of universities. The PVE agenda was established in 2006 as
part of the government's counter-terrorism strategy, which consists of
four main elements:

- Pursue – disrupting terrorists and their operations
- Protect – reducing the vulnerability of UK
- Prepare – prepared for terrorist attack
- Prevent – stopping people becoming terrorists.

PVE was officially defined by the Department for Communities and Local Government (DCLG) as a strategy that aims to stop 'people becoming terrorists or supporting violent extremism', and part of its strategy to build 'strong and positive relationships between people of different backgrounds and a sense of belonging to a shared vision of the future'.

In 2007-8, the Prevent strategy was funded to the tune of £45 million but in 2008/9 the budget was extended to £140 million and a further 300 counter-terrorist officers added across 24 police forces in England (Travis, 2009b). Funded projects include partnerships between police, community and faith groups, mentoring for vulnerable, at risk students and faith awareness weeks in colleges. Also included are English language courses for Imams and Continuing Professional Development courses to teach them about the importance of issues such as child protection.

PVE was launched via series of documents and toolkits aimed at supporting schools, colleges, universities and other public bodies in the task of challenging 'extremist' behaviour, a term which is at the same time both too vaguely and too specifically defined as a problem of Islam. Other forms of extremism are mentioned, such as far-right activism, yet government documents, the DCLG website and political speeches connected to the strategy have consistently taken the line that 'the greatest threat at present [is] from terrorists who claim to act in the name of Islam' (Home Office, 2009:13). The schools and colleges document explicitly states that Al Qaida related activity is the main focus. The Higher Education document adds:

> the government judges the principal current terrorist threat to the UK to be from Islamist terrorism. The threat is international in its scope, involving a variety of individuals, networks and groups who are driven by violent and extremist beliefs. They are indiscriminate – aiming to commit murder and cause mass casualties, regardless of the age, nationality, or religion of their victims and they are prepared to commit suicide to do so. (DIUS, 2006)

PVE has also been supported by contentious militaristic language. 'Winning hearts and minds' was the subtitle of the PVE action plan published by the DCLG in 2007. This was a key slogan of the British, coined in response to the heavy-handed tactics employed by US soldiers in the

Afghanistan war. Underlying PVE is the assumption that all Muslims may be susceptible to condoning terrorism. In Denham's speech in 2009, the earlier notion of 'support' for extremism was further developed into 'tacit' support, including words and deeds that go unchallenged.

> Prevent, as we have designed it, can only work best if the vast majority of Muslims oppose violent extremism. Prevent is all about bringing the power of that majority to bear on the minority who would give the *tacit support* of verbal justification which can create the space in which terrorists recruit and act. (Denham, 2009, emphasis added)

Denham went on to suggest that 'silence can be interpreted as acquiescence or tacit acceptance'. In other words, as Spalek *et al* (2008) point out, the responsible and active Muslim citizen is required to engage in internal community surveillance. If they fail to challenge words and deeds that may be considered to offer support for terrorism, they may themselves be seen as complicit in extremism. Two of the 'partners' or allies of the New Labour government in defeating extremism were women and young Muslims. In 2008, the National Muslim Women's Advisory Group was launched by Gordon Brown. The Young Muslims' Advisory Group was set up to advise government on matters of policy.

However, New Labour's terms of engagement with these groups represented a powerful mix of 'empowerment' and surveillance. References across political speeches and DCLG documents focused on the need to 'give' Muslim women the 'confidence to speak out' but they in turn were expected to monitor community members for signs of extremism. Such references also reflect gendered assumptions about the roles that Muslim women play within their communities. Muslim women were assumed to be routinely oppressed – too fearful to speak out, but also too fearful to expose – the implicit assumption being that women harbour (extremists and terrorists) while men 'do' terrorism.

Educational institutions, too, are seen as having a vital role to play in rooting out this terrorism. Kundnani has argued that there is strong evidence that a significant part of the PVE programme has involved the embedding of counter terrorism police within the delivery of local services such as schools and colleges for the purpose of gathering intelligence on Muslim communities. At the same time as being reminded that they should ideally gain the consent of young people to share information about them, educators and youth workers expressed concerns that they were expected to be the 'eyes and ears' of security policing (Kundnani, 2009).

This mix of consent and coercion, empowerment and surveillance, resonates with wider educational agendas, most notably the significance given to 'pupil voice' through the personalisation agenda (Avis, 2008), which sits alongside authoritarian policies that propose to give headteachers unaccountable powers to exclude students (Jones, 2009).

Since 2006, when the government released its first draft of the universities' document *Promoting Good Campus Relations: Working with Staff and Students to Build Community Cohesion and Tackle Violence in the Name of Islam at Universities and Colleges*, the Higher Education sector has been the subject of controversy. The publication employs language which is 'counter-intuitively authoritarian' (Maughan Brown, 2007), reminding university leaders of the legislative context in which they work – where withholding information from the authorities is a crime under UK law. It provoked anger that universities were required to 'spy on students' (Dodd, 2006)

Promoting Good Campus Relations suggests that university campuses provide an opportunity for already radicalised individuals to form new networks and extend existing ones. It warns against the dangers of permitting external speakers invited by Islamic societies onto campuses, suggesting that such invitees:

> ... can be forceful, persuasive and eloquent. They are able to fill a vacuum created by young Muslims' feelings of alienation from their parents' generation by providing greater 'clarity' from an Islamic point of view on a range of issues, and potentially a greater sense of purpose about how Muslim students can respond. (DIUS, 2009:21)

This repeats familiar themes of culture clash that have dominated policy frameworks relating to Asian and Muslim communities since the 1970s, at the same time as it introduces the discourse of 'grooming' for extremism. And it, too, denies agency to Muslim youth as discussed in the previous section.

Jackson *et al* (2007) observed that this discursive and political-legal context defines the space in which scholars research, think and write about terrorism. In 2006, there was controversy when MI5's Joint Terrorism Analysis Centre (JTAC) tried to fund a research initiative through the Economic and Social Research Council for researchers to 'scope the growth in influence and membership of extremist Islamist groups in the past 20 years ... name key figures and key groups' and 'understand the use of theological legitimisation for violence'. The *Times Higher Education Supplement* observed that the initiative smacked of 'the Cold War use of academics in counter-insurgency activities – essentially using academics as spies' (Baty, 2007).

In 2008, Hicham Yezza, a Nottingham University administrator and researcher, along with student Rizwan Sabir, was arrested under Section 41 of the Terrorism Act 2000, on suspicion of the 'instigation, preparation and commission of acts of terrorism'. He had downloaded an Al Qaida manual for research purposes and the arrests sparked a debate over academic freedom. In 2009, Yezza faced deportation charges over visa irregularities.

In January 2010, it emerged that details of student members of the Islamic society at University College London (UCL) were handed over to police by the university's student union. Special branch officers had visited the campus during their investigation into the attempted bombing in Detroit by Umar Farouk Abdulmutallab on 25 December 2009. Abdulmutallab studied engineering at UCL from 2005 to 2008, and was president of the UCL Islamic Society in 2006-07 (*Independent*, 1 April, 2010).

All this contributes to the rise of what Fekete (2008:102) describes as a 'revamped version of McCarthyism, with its highly public loyalty reviews and congressional hearings ... being injected into the body politic, with particular mutations being developed in particular contexts'.

Teaching and the 'war on terror'

Although the language of the 'war on terror' abated with the Obama – Brown coalition in 2008[7], it continues to impact on the schooling of Muslim children. Little provision has been made for the safeguarding of Muslim pupils, who have been subjected to increased surveillance and harassment.

In 2002, Citizenship Education became a compulsory part of the curriculum for all 11-16 year olds in state maintained schools. The Ajegbo review of *Diversity in the Curriculum* (DfES, 2007b) was commissioned in 2005, in the aftermath of the London bombings and fears about "home grown' terrorism' (Osler, 2009, 2010), but does not mention the 'war on terror'. The review added a fourth pillar: 'Identity and Diversity: Living Together' to the existing three strands of the citizenship curriculum. But, as Osler points out, there is little mention of contemporary racism in its suggested schemes of work. From its inception, Citizenship Education was seen as a possible arena for promoting anti-racist education, but, rather, it has maintained the social control functions associated with the new right's initial attempt to introduce it, in the 1990s). Children are encouraged to be 'good' citizens and to engage with a narrow domestic notion of politics but not to become 'too political' (Osler, 2009). Gillborn (2006) comments that from the start, it was a 'placebo' that was designed to give the illusion of tackling race inequality.

In 2006, Blair argued that 'this country is a blessed nation. The British are special. The World knows it; in our innermost thoughts we know it. This is the greatest nation on earth' (cited in Gillborn, 2008:722). Lee (2006) likewise observed an emerging defence of Empire in Gordon Brown's speeches, quoting Kearney's report in 2005 for the BBC. In this, Brown is reported to have told Kearney's production crew that 'we should be proud ... of the Empire', that 'the days of Britain having to apologise for our history are over', and that 'we should celebrate much of our past rather than apologise for it, and we should talk, rightly so, about British values' (Kearney, 2005). Lee argues that by claiming that the Empire had given Britain a greater global reach than any other country, Brown specifically linked imperialism with enduring British values of enterprise and internationalism and asserted that missionaries have been driven to Africa 'by their own sense of duty' (cited in Lee, 2006).

The theme of Empire featured strongly in the Coalition's Education Secretary Michael Gove's agenda for the history curriculum. In May 2010, he approached the pro-Empire TV historian Niall Ferguson to help rewrite the history curriculum for English schools. Milne (2010b) notes that Ferguson championed British colonialism and stated that 'Empire is more necessary in the 21st century than ever before' and that Andrew

Roberts, who speaks of the British Empire as an 'exemplary force for good', was also approached by the Conservatives (*ibid*).

In October 2010, academic historian Simon Schama became an advisor to Government on the re-shaping of the history curriculum. In his speech to the Conservative party conference, Gove attacked the current approach to history teaching which, he claimed, denied children the opportunity to learn about 'our island story'. Gove asserted that Schama's involvement would inspire pupils to learn a 'narrative British history'. Shama remarked that there is more than one narrative of British history but at the party conference, Gove indicated which narrative should be told through the curriculum:

> Children are growing up ignorant of one of the most inspiring stories I know – the history of our United Kingdom'. ... Our history has moments of pride and shame, but unless we fully understand the struggles of the past we will not properly value the liberties of the present.

Gove was reported to be concerned that the history curriculum for 11 to 13-year-olds included anti-slavery campaigners, William Wilberforce and Olaudah Equiano, but not Winston Churchill. Gove proposed that 'good' British literature: the poetry of Pope and Shelley, the satire of Swift and the novels of Dickens and Hardy, which he defines as the best in the world, should be placed at the heart of the English curriculum. At the conference, with the Union Jack prominent in the background, the Prime Minister told the Coalition members: 'your country needs you'.

The recent appeals to Britishness and Empire need to be seen in the economic and political context. Writing about the contradictions inherent in the New Labour project on race, Back *et al* (2002:450) suggested that its cohesion policies attempted to reconcile an 'aspiration for a model of neo-liberal economic growth, based on a rhetoric of globalised economic forces, with an attempt to protect the social integrity of the nation-state'. Britishness tests, citizenship ceremonies, and Britishness taught on the school curriculum, could be read from this perspective as offering one way of hanging onto a sense of national identity in the face of pressure to compete as a global player. However, these 'inclusive' politics of community cohesion also represent the 'softer' consensual face of a series of coercive measures designed to contain and manage problem populations (Burnett, 2009).

These appeals to Britishness and the history of Empire appear to be part of desperate measures to instill national pride in the British public at a time when Britain's imperial power and status as a leading western economy is being challenged by countries such as China and India. The forging of a renewed British identity can be read in this context as an ideological mechanism to deflect attention from a British economy in decline. Patriotic appeals to a mythic Britishness help to create the illusion of a cohesive society at a time when disadvantage and class inequalities threaten to become stark in consequence of savage cuts to public funding.

Conclusion

Dominant discourses position Muslim boys as underachievers, who face a future of violent criminality or extremism. This chapter has located current concerns about Muslim youth in a policy and historical context and shown how, since the 1960s, successive governments have characterised minorities as problems to be managed and contained. Recent debate at European level has re-positioned poor, disadvantaged Muslim communities as suspect populations in need of surveillance.

Despite the promise of 'equality' and 'fairness', successive governments since the late 1970s have mobilised race through notions of 'community' (Worley, 2005), to justify increasingly coercive state approaches to the management of problem populations.

Tony Blair's notion of modern Britain as united around concepts of community and neighbourhood seemed at first to signal a shift from a Thatcherite model of a divided nation. However, New Labour's policies exacerbated both material and ideological divisions between and within advantaged and disadvantaged communities. Rather than creating a united Britain, New Labour's 'one nation' and the Coalition Government's appeals to 'fairness' in a 'big society' have provided a convenient distraction from the realities of economic downturn and further decline in Britain's global power (Gowan, 2009; Gokay, 2010) that threaten to expose the extent to which the gap between the haves and the have-nots is growing.

> Focusing on those who are excluded from society and coming up with ways of including them in the government's social exclusion strategies shifts

away from inequalities and conflicts of interests amongst those who are excluded and presupposes there is nothing inherently wrong in contemporary society as long as it is made more inclusive through government policies. (McGhee, 2003:393)

At the same time as calling for 'equality' and 'fairness' and integration, recent governments have segregated the communities they seek ostensibly to unite. Such divisions have been sharpened through policies in education which, through the PVE strategy, have become suffused with counter-terrorism and surveillance. This is the context in which the educational experiences of Muslim boys today need to be read.

Notes

1 See for example Abbas' argument about the Tipton three and the Dudley two; see also Appleton's (2001) critique of this research of the causes of fundamentalism 'An old ideology of Islam 'The Fundamentalist question, *Spiked Politics*

2 Conservative minister Edward Boyle suggested that the numbers of ethnic minority children should be limited to 15 per cent in any one school, in the interests of maintaining a quality education for indigenous white children (Grosvenor, 1997)

3 See for example Deborah Orr's analysis (*Independent*, 5 March, 2005); Boris Johnson's piece 'The Shabina Begum case never had anything to do with modesty' in the *Telegraph*, 23 March, 2006; 'Jasper Gerard meets Shabina Begum Faith, the veil, shopping and me' *The Sunday Times* 26 March, 2006; Dilpazier Aslam 'I could scream with happiness. I've given hope and strength to Muslim women' (*Guardian*, 3 March, 2005

4 Joanna Gilmore (2010), a researcher at Manchester University, asserts that police reportedly told Muslim families to keep their sons off the streets 'otherwise they will be arrested' when an EDL march was announced in Burnley in July 2010 – exposing the link between engaging in legal protests and the risk of criminalisation

5 David Blunkett's speeches in the aftermath of the inner city disturbances in 2001 called on Muslims to abandon such practices

6 Blair's 'Duty to Integrate' speech (2006); see also Blears (2009)

7 After the failed bomb attacks in 2007, Gordon Brown is said to have developed new guidelines for ministers, directing them to 'drop' the 'war on terror' language' and 'banning' them from connecting Muslims with terrorist attacks due to concerns of undermining cohesion (Daily Express, 2007); there was also a shift in language adopted by the Home Secretary in 2008 when she referred to alleged terrorist activities as anti-Islamic activity (*Daily Mail*, 17 January 2008); in 2007 (*Guardian*, 17 January), David Milliband described the government's use of the 'war on terror' terminology as 'a mistake'

2

Setting the scene: theorising and researching youth experiences

Introduction

We see that how working class Muslim boys who are located in some of the most economically deprived areas of England have come to be defined socially and culturally as the new folk devils. Chapters three to seven examine how the boys I interviewed encounter, define and negotiate the material and cultural conditions of their existence in the context of schooling and their local environment, and the resources and strategies they employ to deal with their experiences. The search for strategies and resources concerns structure, agency and resistance – with which sociologists of youth and education have long been occupied. This chapter briefly reviews some of the ways in which sociologists of youth have addressed issues of agency within structural constraints since the 1970s before outlining key concepts and positions that are central to my own understandings of these issues. It then discusses recent research on young Muslims in a post 9/11 context and ends with an outline of the empirical study explored in the following chapters.

Theorising youth experiences: key concepts and positions

In much of the early theorising of youth experiences, ethnic minority youth were either invisible or marginalised to the status of victims, as in Pearson's (1976) subcultural study of 'Paki-bashing'. Within the dominant field of ethnicity studies in the 1970s, they tended to be characterised as victims of cultural and religious practices. This section briefly reviews these research traditions before outlining the key theoretical concepts and positions on which the book draws.

Subculture

Since the 1970s sociologists of youth and education have attempted to research the ways in which young people make sense of the situations they find themselves in. The pioneering studies of the Birmingham Centre for Contemporary Cultural Studies (CCCS) remain a central reference point for youth research, most notably the landmark study, *Resistance Through Rituals* conducted by Hall and Jefferson in 1976. This research was conducted in reaction to both the dominant thesis of class-less youth (Abrams, 1959; Coleman, 1966) and the economic crisis in the 1970s which gave rise to new moral panics concerning young people. Hall and Jefferson argued that the youth culture thesis disguised the class basis of youth experiences, so deflecting attention from the material conditions that differentially shaped young people's cultural experiences. Taking Marx's dialectical analysis, that people are formed and form themselves through culture and history, Hall and Jefferson defined culture as:

> ... [that] level at which groups develop distinct patterns of life and give 'expressive form' to their social and material existence ... Culture is the way the social relations of a group are structured and shaped: but it is also the way those shapes are experienced, understood and interpreted. (1976:11)

Just as groups and classes stand in rank order to one another, so cultures are differently ranked. Cultures, however, do not stand in direct opposition to one another; they coexist. Drawing on Gramsci (1971), Hall and Jefferson argued that the dominant culture was not completely homogenous, nor complete, since divisions existed between various sections which can have opposing interests. There was therefore always space for other cultures to challenge or resist their cultural hegemony. Gramsci's concept of hegemony refers to power and leadership, principally achieved through consent, but with coercion always in reserve. By adopting the concept of hegemony, Gramsci drew attention to the role of culture (institutionalised for example, in the church, the family, the law, or education, arts and media), in the organisation of power in societies. He argued that the maintenance of hegemony requires economic, political and cultural domination so that class struggle involves the battle for ideas, as well as the struggle for state and economic power.

It followed for Hall and Jefferson that ideological or cultural resistance was a key form of political activity, since hegemony is never complete. For these authors deviant youth styles in the form of 'subcultures' presented a challenge to the hegemony of the state. The term subculture was defined by Hall and Jefferson in terms of its relationship to the parent culture and more widely in terms of its relationship with the dominant culture. Subcultures were, 'sub-sets – smaller, more localised and differentiated structures, within one or other of the larger cultural networks (p13). Subcultures, however, were not simply 'ideological constructs':

> They, too, win space for the young: cultural space in the neighbourhood and institutions, real time for leisure and recreation, actual room on the street or street corner. They serve to mark out and appropriate 'territory' in the localities. They focus around key occasions of social interaction: the weekend, the disco, the bank holiday trip, the night out in the 'centre', and 'stand-about-doing-nothing' of the weekday evening, the Saturday match. (Hall and Jefferson, 1976:45-6)

This and subsequent work (eg Corrigan, 1979; Willis, 1977) therefore looked to culture and everyday life for signs of class conflict and resistance, essentially how young people 'made sense' of the situations in which they found themselves. As Nayak argues (2003:16), this reading presented subcultural practices as:

> 'rituals of resistance' enacted by working class youth in response to the break-up of traditional communities and an unbridled post-war consumerism that was creating a sharply visible, unequal distribution of wealth. (Nayak, 2003:16)

Willis's (1977) seminal study of the transition from school to work offered a further nuanced elaboration of the concept of cultural resistance. Willis studied twelve working class 'lads' concentrating on their attempts to win cultural space because of boredom and blocked opportunities and alienation. The 'lads' formed their own culture, which ran counter to the dominant culture of the school, but parallel to 'shopfloor' culture. There was a direct relationship between the counter-culture found in the school and that of the shop floor in terms of the strategies adopted by both, and the shared focal concerns of 'toughness', 'machismo', 'independence' and 'enjoyment'. The 'lads' played an active part in their own failure by resisting the very thing which school has to offer them – knowledge. According to Willis, the lads failed to turn their symbolic victory into a real victory, so that by the time they reach the factory there is only recognition and not surprise. Willis demonstrated that this was part of the process of the regeneration and reproduction of working class culture, and the conditions of its oppression.

Critiquing subculture

Feminist critiques (McRobbie and Garber, 1976; Smart, 1976; Cain, 1981; Cambell, 1981; Heidensohn, 1985; Griffin, 1986; Leonard, 1987; McRobbie, 1991) of early subcultural theories focused on the inherent masculinism of youth subcultural research and the invisibility or marginal treatment of girls and women. This was because of an exclusive focus on white working class and heterosexual males. While these studies focused on white girls and young women, studies of black youth subcultures (Hall, 1980; Gilroy, 1982, 1987) also concentrated almost exclusively (though see Fuller, 1982) on African-Caribbean males – women and other ethnic minorities were excluded.

One of the reasons for the 'invisibility' of girls to these 1970s and 1980s youth cultural studies related to the gendered specific and segregated forms of leisure adopted by young people. While young men occupied the masculine worlds of the street, young women were confined to the privatised 'bedroom cultures' of the home, creating consequent methodological difficulties with researching young women (McRobbie, 1991).

Delamont (2000) also criticises the romanticism with which young men were viewed by male sociologists:

> The anti-school delinquent, rebellious young working class urban males have been lovingly chronicled and even celebrated as heroes, although they epitomise everything no sociologists would actually want to live next door to in real life and are the embodiment of the opposite of the social mobility grand narrative which produced the sociologists. Most of the male sociologists who have lovingly chronicled the rebellion and resistances of the hooligans to schooling are themselves the heroic products of the social mobility and narrative of their sub discipline. They worked hard at school, did their homework, passed exams, took the advice of teachers, went to

> university and became academics. They 'lived' the vision of the Fabians, embodied the narrative of Halsey, Heath and Ridge (1980). However, once middle-class, they have not only studied, but lionised the very type of boys from whom they had to hide in the playground. (Delamont, 2000:99)

A further criticism of subcultural studies related to the methodology and the tendency in some accounts (eg Hebdige, 1979) to 'read off' the experiences of young people from various signs without interrogating 'lived' experiences (Back, 1996; Nayak, 2003). The all-embracing concept of class resistance has also been subjected to critique for not specifying clearly what was being resisted or for reading individual acts of deviance as evidence of class resistance (see Gewirtz, 1991).

One strand of youth research has, since the late 1980s, rejected the concept of youth subculture altogether in favour of a focus on club cultures, tribes or youthscapes (Skelton and Valentine, 1997; Bennet, 1999). However, the core focus on culture (peer groups, teacher-pupil interactions, school texts) has remained pivotal to ethnographic studies of black youth (Fuller, 1982; Mac an Ghaill, 1988, 1994; Connolly, 1988; Mirza, 1992; Sewell, 1997; Archer, 2003; Shain, 2003). Nayak's (2003) study of white working class youth in the northeast of England retains the concept of subculture but also emphasises the need to locate subcultural responses within a wider analysis of local and school contexts.

Culture clash

Studies in the 1970s which focused primarily on African-Caribbean and Asian youth from within the Ethnicity School tradition (Watson, 1976; Khan, 1977) were often framed within a culture clash perspective which pathologised the experiences of Asian youth. This perspective placed their experiences in a frame of intergenerational conflict between their parents, who imposed strict traditional upbringing on them, and the youth who desired a western life style. In addition, gendered discourses positioned boys as the heirs of patriarchal privilege and girls as victims of static and fixed patriarchal cultures (Alexander, 2000). The exclusive focus on ethnicity in this body of work also lacked reference to wider historical and material conditions. Much of this literature presented the experiences of Asian youth without reference to the broader social and historical framework that accounts for the subordination of black groups in Britain (Lawrence, 1982; Fryer, 1985, 1988). In a wider critique of the ethnicity school literature, Miles argued (1982:64) that using the concept of ethnicity to refer to the perception of group difference made the term refer to any criteria by which a group might distinguish itself from another and that, secondly, an exclusive emphasis on cultural difference served to conceal the economic, political and ideological conditions that allow the attribution of meaning.

The CCCS also argued:

> Culture is seen as an autonomous realm which merely intersects with other social processes. The effect of this is to produce a static and idealised vision of Asian cultures, which cannot really take account of class caste, regional differences and which cannot help us to understand how and why those 'cultures' have changed. (CCCS, 1981:113-114)

Shifting identities: race, class and gender in articulation

Since the 1980s, sociologists of youth and education (Mirza, 1992; Haw, 1994; Basit, 1997; Connolly, 1998; Dwyer, 1999; Archer, 2003; Shain, 2003) have challenged the fixed and static conceptions of culture found in both the ethnicity school literature and the class reductionism characteristic of early subcultural studies of youth. They have drawn on alternative theoretical frameworks from neo-Marxist, postcolonial and poststructuralist theorising (Hall, 1980, 1992, 1996; Brah and Minhas, 1986; Bhavnani and Phoenix, 1994; Brah, 1996) to argue for a focus on the complex reality of the lived experiences of young people. Drawing on postcolonial and poststructural accounts of identities as multiple and constantly negotiated, such research has instead emphasised the complex interrelationship between capitalist, patriarchal and imperialist relations as structures of power that shape the experiences of young people.

Heidi Mirza (1992), for example, argued that African-Caribbean girls' experiences of education were formulated within a colonial narrative which embedded Eurocentric and racist elements of capitalism and imperialism. She focuses on the family as the centrepiece for challenging the dominant conceptions of black girls that position them as lacking self-esteem compared with confident middle class girls.

Research on British-born Asian and Muslim youth (Dwyer, 1999; Archer, 2003; Shain, 2003; Bhopal, 2010) has focused on the more active role played by them in negotiating identities based on both residual 'home' cultures and the local cultures they currently inhabit. Such research challenges the additive and double and triple subordination model as that were applied in the 1970s and 1980s to theorising racialised experiences and identities. Additive models amounted to a race plus gender plus class approach which failed to recognise the multiple ways in which these variables interact or intersect to produce specifically classed, racialised and gendered experiences. This latter intersectionality approach also emphasises the interlocking of patriarchal, capitalist and imperial relations in ways that structure and shape, but do not determine, the experiences of young people (Shain, 2003).

Religion, 'race' and masculine identities
Since the 1990s, literature has noted an increasing propensity among young Muslims to draw on religion as a marker of identity (Knott and Khoker, 1993; Haw, 1994; Dwyer, 1999; Mirza, 1999; Saeed *et al*, 1999; Werbner, 1996, 2005; Archer, 2003). Studies of Muslim girls' schooling (Knott and Khoker, 1993; Haw, 1994; Dwyer, 1999; Mirza, 1999) highlighted the girls' positive assertions of Muslim identities that challenged fixed and static conceptions of Asian cultures and culture clash frameworks. Research on Muslim boys and young men has focused on radicalisation and the performance of Muslim masculinities.

Radicalisation
The attempt to understand young people's increased identifications with Islam pre-dates the terrorist attack of September 11, 2001, but policy and academic literature has since exploded (Glees and Pope, 2005; Leppard and Fielding, 2005; Buijs *et al*, 2006; Abbas, 2007; Choudhury, 2007; Spalek, 2007). Earlier theorisations of the political mobilisations around the Rushdie affair focused on factors other than religion. Samad (1992) emphasised the material disadvantage experienced by a largely Mirpuri working class community which had suffered from a decade of racist provocations. Various organisations, such as the Azad Kashmir Muslim Association and the Asian Youth Movement, had persistently argued during the late 1970s that racial tension in Bradford was increasing, as was the activity of the British National Party, the National Front and the Yorkshire Campaign to Stop Immigration.

The case of the Bradford 12[1] and the Honeyford[2] affair became powerful push factors among the young Mirpuris who were searching for outlets to voice their discontent. Samad argues that the young Pakistanis' hurt at *The Satanic Verses*, which they perceived as another gratuitous insult, exacerbated the anger lingering after the Honeyford affair. As Samad argues, 'it was the perception that they were again humiliated which was responsible for making religious consciousness dominant over identities' (1992:516).

Modood (1992) maintained that the demonstrations and book burning were, above all, working class anger and hurt pride. But his explanation for this anger taking a religious outlet – his argument was that these young people had been deserted by a secular intelligentsia which did not understand or feel responsible for its own working class – has been criticised. Glynn, on the other hand, argues that, 'there is certainly a vacuum and a lack of secular leadership but that vacuum is not due to the absence of a middle-class, which would hardly be expected to breach the gap of class experience' (2001:977). Like Nira Yuval Davis (1992), Glynn identifies the 'turn to religion' as a consequence of the demise of socialism with the collapse of the former eastern bloc. She argues that when people no longer see socialism as being able to offer a way out, working class anger will turn to other movements. Yuval Davis argued that 'in the third world, and among third world minorities in the west, the rise of fundamentalism is intimately linked with the failure of nationalist and socialist movements to bring successful liberation from oppression, exploitation and poverty (1992:280).

I have argued that theories of radicalisation, following the 2005 London transport bombing and the attempted terrorist attacks in London and Scotland, have been based much more strongly on the individual and detailed accounts of processes that may lead individuals to turn to religion. Choudhury (2007) argues that identity politics can turn into radicalisation when shaped by external factors such as the disparagement of Muslims by governments, and their internal empowerment.

Performing Muslim masculinities

In contrast to dominant representations of Muslim boys as disaffected and at risk of radicalisation – a thesis supported in the radicalisation theories discussed in the last chapter, recent sociological research suggests that Muslim boys and young men may strategically take up (Archer, 2003) or reject (Hopkins, 2006, 2007) Muslim identities to challenge dominant stereotypes of weak Asian passivity. At the same time they may make investments in Islamic cultural capital to support a bid for patriarchal power in the face of declining economic capital (Dwyer, 1999; Macey, 1999; Hopkins, 2006; Ramji, 2007). This research draws on the concept of multiple and relational masculinities (Connell, 1987, 1995) that are embedded in institutional practices and also embodied in gender practices (Swain, 2002). Masculinity is understood as multiple, constantly repositioned and contested in ongoing performances. The hegemonic form of masculinity (Connell, 1995, 1997) is not necessarily the most common type but is often underwritten by the threat of violence. It therefore has the capacity to portray itself as the natural order of things, and many boys find that they have to fit into it and conform to its demands. This hegemony works by consent (Swain, 2002). Thus, masculinities are simultaneously constructed in relation to their classed locations (prospect of unemployment), patriarchy (dominance over women), Islamophobia (anti-Muslim racism) and cultural stereotyping of Muslim boys as dangerous fanatics.

Louise Archer (2003) conducted discussion group interviews with 31 Muslim boys aged 14-15 in a northern mill town in the mid-1990s. Drawing on feminist poststructuralism and a discourse analytic approach, she argued that the boys take up a range of masculinities in different contexts. For example, Muslim masculinities were drawn on by the boys in her study to resist notions of 'weak' Asian masculinity, which had in the past been equated with passivity. However, the boys drew on patriarchal Asian identities and asserted their privilege as males. In the context of local identities, they drew on popular black cultural forms represented through 'gangsta' masculinities. Archer (2003: 50) argues that:

> The boys' construction of a 'strong' Muslim brotherhood might be usefully read in terms of the intertwining of racial and patriarchal themes, through which boys resist popular stereotypes of 'weak' and 'passive' Asian masculinity. The boys' identifications could be seen as straightforwardly challenging this stereotype, replacing it with an alternative association of Muslim masculinity with strength. The boys' association between Muslim identity, unity and strength challenge contemporary western ideals of

individualistic white masculinity and elsewhere. The boys differentiated between strong, collective Muslim families and unstable highly individualistic western/white family structure.

Hopkins (2006, 2007) conducted focus group discussions and individual interviews with 55 Muslim males in Scotland aged 16-25. His sample was older and more middle class than Archer's. Hopkins found that his respondents took up a range of identity positions between different intersecting scales, sometimes asserting their identities as 'local' through neighbourhood relations and as 'nationalists' through a strong appeal to Scottish nationalism. At other times they drew on and sometimes rejected global Muslim identities through spiritual connection to the *umma*. The *umma* represents a global Muslim brotherhood.

Hopkins found that the young men's identifications were contradictory: they argued that men and women are equal in Islam, whilst simultaneously advocating sexist stereotypes about their expectations of Muslim women. Hopkins refers to this as 'sexist equality' and sees it as supporting Linda McDowell's (2002:115) findings that young men's masculinities are constructed around a belief in 'domestic conformity' whereby young men focus on earning wages and reproducing sexist and heterosexual familial situations. Dwyer (2000:479) too notes that this policing by the young men appeared to be a means by which they could maintain their own adolescent masculine ethnic and religious identity.

This theme of patriarchal control through Muslim masculinities is taken further by Ramji (2007), who draws on Bourdieu's concepts of capital and field to analyse investments in Islamic identity by young Muslims. Ramji argues that the mobilisation of religion is often ambivalent, contradictory and intersected with social differences, particularly class. The Muslim men in her study drew on three main discourses to legitimate patriarchal power. They saw themselves as the main providers for their families and they cited the Quran and *Hadith* to support this. Their ability to provide was directly related to enabling Muslim women to observe their 'duty' to maintain Islamic 'modesty' – that was the responsibility of Muslim women to uphold. The key markers of modesty were wearing *hijab* and abstaining from paid work.

Ramji's third theme concerned relationships: the Asian Muslim masculinity evidenced in her interviews placed a high level of attachment to displays of heterosexual prowess. The mobilisation of Islamic modesty was used by the men (all of whom displayed heterosexual identities), to decode which girls deserved respect and were 'sisters' and which girls could be approached for 'a date'. She found that Islam was mobilised by her respondents to secure the basis of a superior status for themselves as Muslim men, a superiority not readily available in other aspects of their lives. An Islamic identity in which they enjoyed superiority was powerful cultural capital for the Muslim men interviewed; it could counteract their lack of economic, social and symbolic capital in British society. Religion could thus be a resource for securing a dominant gender identity. This was particularly important when access to other capital was limited because of racism and other prejudice. Ramji considered young men's investments in Islamic cultural capital to be a reaction to the growing educational divide between themselves and Muslim women. Class seemed to influence how this was voiced. The working-class Muslim men interviewed had less access to economic capital and so relied on religion to give them access to a cultural capital, which could then be converted to other capital such as social, or indeed economic if it created a situation where only men are allowed to work.

The complex catalogue of shifting and strategic identifications indicated in these studies of young Muslim men suggests a need to move beyond prevailing discourses of Asian gangs (Alexander, 2000) and beyond the popular and academic theorisations of radicalisation which position Muslim boys as disaffected and alienated from both their local cultures and processes of local democracy. The current study sets out to do this by exploring the strategic take up of various identities in order to deal with or make sense of the local predicaments. As we see in chapters three to seven, the boys sometimes globalised their local predicaments by drawing on strong assertive and collective global Muslim identities, while at other times they were fiercely local in their identifications and struggles over neighbourhood identities. Thus as Archer (2003:53-5) argues, 'the boundaries of Muslim identity were constantly negotiated and contested within the discussion groups and the boys asserted, resisted and justified various positioning of themselves within or outside particular boundaries'.

Theorising identities

The approach taken in this book is that structures of race, gender and class are cross-cutting and produced in 'articulation', that is, in the inter-section of everyday lives with economic and political relations of domination and subordination. For Gramsci this articulation is:

> ...the starting point of critical elaboration: it is the consciousness of what one really is, and knowing thyself' as a product of the historical processes to date which deposited an infinity of traces, without leaving an inventory ... each individual is a synthesis not only of existing relations but of the history of these relations ... a précis of the past. (Gramsci, cited in Ruther-ford, 1990:20)

Gramsci's framework recognises that young people are located in material contexts which constrain and structure the limits of possi-bilities for agency and action. This entails recognition of the role of his-torical forces – in this case of colonialism and imperialism – in shaping the class locations and settlement patterns of Muslim communities in areas of England that have suffered most from economic decline. These settlement patterns have had a lasting legacy in terms of the types of schooling and educational and employment opportunities available. Pakistani and Bangladeshi communities find themselves located in some of the most materially deprived wards in the country.

These poor, disadvantaged communities have also been subject to dominant racialised and classed, cultural definitions of them as 'lack-ing', 'deficient' and responsible for their own marginality. Discourses of integration position Muslim communities as insular and isolationist. Through discourses of the 'war on terror' Muslim boys have been de-fined as dangerous, suspect and vulnerable (to extremism) and thus as a threat to the British nation. However, these dominant cultural read-ings are hegemonic (Gramsci, 1971) – dominant but constantly chal-lenged in and through local contexts, sometimes in ways that reinforce dominant stereotypes of violent masculinity, as we saw over the so-called riots in 2001.

Schooling is an important mediator of dominant discourses and defini-tions of Muslim and Asian students. It is the major public site for the active negotiation of young people's identities where these are con-tested and worked out on a daily basis. I see Muslim boys' identities as produced through an ongoing negotiation between internal and external definitions of identities or 'modes of being' (Brah, 1996). External or objective definitions derive from complex interrelationships between various structural factors (race, religion, class and gender) in particular local, social and historical contexts. Internal definitions of identities relate to the young people's subjective experiences of these situations. Boys may subjectively experience and define their current locations in different ways, depending on how they are positioned and position themselves in relation to dominant discourses. According to Davies and Harre,

> Positioning is the discursive process whereby selves are located in conversations as observable and subjectively coherent participants in jointly produced story lines. There can be interactive positioning in which what one person says positions another. And there can be reflexive positioning in which what one person positions oneself. (1998:48)

The chapters that follow explore the various ways in which Muslim boys in the research study were able to take up and position themselves in relation to dominant discourses of schooling and cultural definitions of them as newly dangerous and suspect in the context of the 'war on terror'.

The empirical study

The research was conducted between May 2002 and October 2003 in Oldwych in the West Midlands. Group and individual interviews were conducted with 24 working class Muslim boys aged 12-18. At the time Oldwych had a population of around 250,000. The proportion of ethnic minorities including Irish was around 6 per cent but around 8 per cent for under 16s. Ethnic minorities were overwhelmingly concentrated in two wards, Newtown and Belstone, where they made up almost 50 per cent of the population. Ryton and Ashfields also contained ethnic minority populations. Like many of the wards in the northern towns, these areas were severely economically deprived. Newtown also had a significant concentration of asylum-seekers, and this had and has been a focal issue of British National Party organisation in the city.

Manufacturing accounted for around 35 per cent of employment in Oldwych, with its main industries – iron, steel and ceramics – in decline. The last mine closed in the mid-1980s and the steelworks soon after, leaving older men to take jobs in the public or service sectors and younger men to opt for university or the dole. Its ceramics industry was still active at the time of the research but losing out to growing competition in the global market place for cheaper production. Men who had previously been employed in these industries were taking up jobs as taxi drivers or working in service industries.

As Kundnani (2001) has observed, Pakistanis and Bangladeshis have not been able to take up public service sector employment because of discrimination and a lack of skills. This was true of Oldwych, where a generation of workers had lived with unemployment and economic uncertainty. This lack of economic stability also explains the strong take up of higher education among Pakistani and Bangladeshi communities as a way out of the social stagnation they are in (Modood, 2007).

Oldwych is recognised as an economically deprived area. It has a higher than average number of people claiming housing benefit and of children eligible for free school meals. At the time of the research, unemployment was around 5.9 per cent – against an average of 4.9 per cent for Britain overall. In Newtown this figure was far higher: 8.6 per cent.

Fieldwork was conducted at two sites: a youth group located in Newtown, in Ryton where boys met once a week, and a mixed 11-16 comprehensive secondary school, Leyton High. The book draws on the accounts of 24 boys, who were interviewed individually and in groups across the two sites. During the first focus group in Newtown, I was accompanied by a male researcher (BG) but I conducted all the other interviews alone. I also spoke to staff across both sites and formally interviewed one of the youth workers.

Seventeen of the boys were Pakistani, including one who described himself as mixed-race white English and Pakistani. Four were Bengali, two were Afghani and one Turkish. Yacoub, a Newtown youth worker, described himself as British Pakistani. Most of the Newtown boys were students at Leyton but some attended other schools, most notably nearby Greenbank school, an 11-16 mixed comprehensive. Two of the boys attended a college of further education in Ryton.

The Newtown youth group was in theory open to all but in reality only Muslim boys attended. As we see in chapter five, the boys complained bitterly about encountering racism when they tried to attend other clubs but they themselves were content to exclude girls. At Leyton, the percentage of ethnic minorities was relatively small at just 11 per cent. This had declined from around 20 per cent in previous years, reportedly because of the high incidence of racialised fighting. The number of students achieving 5 A*-C grades at Leyton was just under 30 per cent, compared with a national average of 52 per cent at the time. In the previous year the figure had been 35 per cent and in subsequent years it has risen to well over 58 per cent but is still significantly lower than the national average.

At Greenbank school, around 39 per cent of students achieved five A-C GCSE grades in the year in which the research was conducted, again lower than the national average. Fixed term exclusion rates were high in both schools with, for example, 133 incidents of exclusion involving 78 pupils and three permanent exclusions in Leyton the year before.

The boys were all from working class backgrounds and most of their fathers were either unemployed, driving a taxi, or employed in the service industry. Three of the families owned restaurant businesses. Only two of the mothers were in full time professional employment, and three boys were living in single parent households, two of them headed by women and one by a man.

The chapters that follow discuss the ways in which boys responded to their material, geographical and cultural locations and consider how their responses demonstrated collective and individual agency in their take up and performance of a range of masculine identity strategies.

Notes

1 In 1981 twelve youths of Indian and Pakistani origin were arrested for being in possession of incendiary devices. Defendants claimed that the petrol bombs were for self-defence against the threatened skinhead attack on their community. Samad relates that their 'trial drew a graphic picture of a community under constant fear of attack, with hardly any offer of police protection' (Samad, 1992:512). The defendants were proved innocent.

2 Ray Honeyford was the Headteacher of Drummond Middle School in Bradford, who made inflammatory assertions, particularly about the Mirpuri community, during the 1980s.

3

'Muslim first': religion, politics and schooling

Introduction

This chapter focuses on the themes of religion and politics in the context of Muslim boys' schooling and identity. As already discussed, the discourse of parallel lives, which is embedded in government cohesion strategies, positions Muslims as isolationist and self-segregating, refusing to integrate or rejecting British citizenship and identity. Young people in general are currently characterised through citizenship agendas as disaffected, disengaged from the processes of local democracy and in need of political literacy. However, discourses of radicalisation emerging from the 'war on terror' position working class Muslim boys as one of the groups most vulnerable to political alienation and therefore at risk of 'extremism'. This is largely because it is assumed that they are more likely to find their opportunities blocked as a result of underachievement or discrimination in the labour market.

This chapter examines the ways in which these wider discourses on Muslim masculinity were mediated by Muslim boys' experiences of schooling and particularly how the boys positioned themselves in relation to these discourses. The first section focuses on self-definitions, setting the context for a discussion of the different strategies the boys draw on to deal with their experiences of schooling and their local environments. It explores the impact of the 'war on terror' on schooling

55

and the strategic take-up of Muslim identities to counter the wide-spread demonisation of Muslims the boys experienced through media coverage of the 'war on terror' and in their schooling and local neigh-bourhood interactions.

'Muslim first': religion and identity

Recent empirical studies on second and third generation British south Asians have noted an increasing tendency among British Pakistanis and Bangladeshis to assert Muslim identities (Eade, 1990, 1994; Werbner, 1996; Samad, 1998; Saeed *et al*, 1999; Archer, 2003; Ramji, 2007). For Samad (1998:204) this 'turn to religion' does not signal an increase in religiosity but rather a 're-working of ethnicity' in response to the public demonisation of Muslims since the Rushdie affair. Recent research suggests that identification with the *umma* – or global collective Islamic brotherhood – represents a form of empowerment enabling for example, Muslim women to mobilise discourses of Islam to counter patriarchal restrictions around marriage and education (Mirza, 1992; Haw, 1996; Dwyer, 1999).

Research on Muslim boys suggests that identification with a global Islamic identity through the concept of *umma* can be a source of em-powerment for boys (Archer, 2003) to counter dominant notions of Asian passivity. Hopkins (2006), however, found that some young men in his study resisted the *umma* in favour of national discourses eg Scottishness and Britishness, while at the same time identifying with global cultural markers such as black cultural forms, but that they could also challenge the dualistic representations of Muslim men as either violent and dangerous or passive and studious.

The majority of Pakistani and Bangladeshi boys in this study took up 'Muslim first' (Naber, 2005) identities with Bengali, Pakistani, Asian and British identities as secondary. Tariq was alone in taking up a British first, Muslim second, identity. He saw Britishness as a citizenship issue because 'I was born here, I've lived here all my life'. This concurs with the findings of research indicating that Britishness is more a legal entitle-ment for ethnic minorities than a statement of ethnicity or identity (Archer, 2003; Ansari, 2004). Farood and Ibrahim were the most recent arrivals to England and, despite their strong associations and inclusion within a dominant Asian boys group in their school (see chapter four), defined themselves first as Afghani and Turkish respectively and second as Muslim. Sajid was the only boy who self-defined only as 'Asian'. Drawing on a biological and fixed notion of ethnicity, his justification was that it was 'like just the way I've been brung up. You've got to live the way you were born'.

Significantly, none of the boys self-identified as English and this matches the findings of research nationally. For example, the Office for National Statistics (cited in Burdsey, 2007:16) found, in 2004, that 67 per cent of Bangladeshis saw themselves as British only, and only 6 per cent identified as English. Other research shows that half of British Asians classify themselves as British and not English (*ibid*) for various reasons, one of which relates to the exclusionary nature of popular manifestations of Englishness (Gilroy, 1993; Back, 1996). One participant in Eade's research (1994) with Bengali Muslims said, 'I don't know why. I just feel to be British, you don't actually have to be white, but to be English I always have this feeling that you have to be white (cited in Burdsey, 2007:16). In line with these sentiments, none of the boys saw themselves as English and some actively rejected Englishness as an identity. As Aziz said, 'I'm not English I have like a British passport', Zahid also rejected Englishness:

> First of all, I'm Muslim. After that I'm Pakistani. I wouldn't like to describe myself as English although I was born in this country. I always thought that after my education was complete, I would go back to Pakistan to live there. (Zahid)

Zahid here invokes a 'myth of return' (Anwar, 1986) more commonly associated with first and second generation ethnic minorities than with third and fourth generations like the boys in the current study. Later, we see that Zahid's rejection of Englishness was centred on a difference that was constructed in relation to a notion of respect. English people did not, according Zahid, have 'enough' respect to look after their elders.

The 'really religious' boys

Zahid was also one of the boys who identified themselves as 'really religious'. Not only did he dissociate himself from Englishness but also from the other Muslim boys in his school (Leyton).

Zahid: What it is, I'm a different kind of person. I don't hang around with people who are nowadays are not very good.
Nowadays most people everybody's not very good. They all smoke drink, everything even though they are Muslims, they still do it. But I'm not that kind of person, I hang around with people who think, who I think, they're good. So, I mostly like, I only go out at the weekends. I mostly, after I go home, I read Quran for some time, then I do my school work. I revise then read namaz and then go to mosque. Weekdays I don't go; I go at the weekend

FS: So, that's important is it, what people do and how they behave?

Zahid: Basically everybody's forgotten like they're Pakistani and where their real background is. This is England now, this is. I'm not like that. I'll never forget it

FS: Ok, so are there any people that you really avoid mixing with?

Zahid: Yeah there are some

FS: What kind of people would they be?

Zahid: They're just like ... they're not like really, really bad: they drink, they smoke, they smoke weed. I don't know what else they do cos I've never really been out with ... they might do things like that I'm not sure ... I know for a fact that they do these things, drink smoke and all that ... and I wouldn't like to drink. If I mixed with them I might think I might try it. I might like to try it

According to Zahid, Muslim – mainly Pakistani – boys in the school identifying as Muslims at the time were engaged in practices such as drinking and smoking, which are considered to be un-Islamic. By contrast, Zahid presents himself as authentically Muslim because of his avoidance of such activities, using the religious discourse of temptation. He suggests that if he tried these activities he might be tempted to join in and therefore leave behind his truly religious identity. However, as we see later, Zahid also presented as academically highly aspirational and his arguments about temptation, couched here in religious terms, also relate to his need to dissociate himself from a group of mainly Pakistani and Bangladeshi boys who were labelled as troublemakers and gang members, in order to maintain his academic reputation among teachers.

Other boys also positioned themselves as 'really religious', including Farood, Rafiq and Arif. They, like Zahid, were also relatively high achievers. The most common markers for the boys being really religious were: praying five times a day, abstaining from romantic relationships and reading the Quran regularly, ideally every day. Really religious boys also policed the boundaries of Islamic modesty, for example:

> My mate Umar over there, he goes [to mosque] five times a day. Not inside school he's all you know ... you don't know him from inside but outside he looks religious. If you like talk about girls he'll just says 'Oi Besharram' [without shame] [both laugh] and that's it. (Shahid)

The boys made reference to Umar's disapproval of the talk and practice of heterosexual relationships. Although they expressed their disapproval through humour, this was a regulatory device that served to monitor and police the boundaries of Islamic modesty. The main effect of this regulation was that the boys did not talk openly about their relationships with girls. Rafiq also strongly disapproved of boys having romantic relationships, suggesting that the boys paid little heed to Islamic codes of conduct. 'Well people in this school don't give a c**p about that. They just go out with white girls. Well I haven't been out with no one and I don't want to either' (Rafiq).

Although virtually all the boys defined themselves as Muslim, it is clear from the accounts so far that the active take up of religiosity varied. Several boys defined themselves as 'not good enough' Muslims in relation to the really 'religious boys'. For example, Aziz talks here about his family's attempts to turn him into a 'better' Muslim:

Aziz: I read *Quran* but I don't read much namaz. I fast and that, but I swear a lot. I do a lot of wrong things basically which I shouldn't do ... I know a lot of information and what I should do and I still do it ... it's just a habit ... my mum shouts at me a lot, my sister shouts at me a lot and my older brother, he doesn't shout but he gives me lecture about it. They force me to read the Quran after school I read all the *namaz* [prayers] but not the morning one. My sister tries to wake me up but I can't. So I don't really do much

            ***

FS: Are you religious?

59

Abid:	As in like prayer? I don't really. What, are you Muslim? [FS: yes] I do *Zuhr* and *Asar* but *Ishah* it's too tiring. It's like 11 o'clock. I try
FS:	Do you go to the mosque ever?
Abid:	[laughs shaking head]. I do go to *Jumma* [Friday prayers] when I've got holiday and when it's Ramadan I go nearly every day

***

FS:	Do you go to mosque ever?
Sajid:	Yes
FS:	Is that because you want to or have to?
Sajid:	No I just want to really, just with my mates when we've nothing to do. We're all bored [and] we just say let's go mosque or something

Aziz's account suggests a strong family pressure to conform to religious requirements against which he reads himself as a 'failed Muslim'. This supports on one level the cultural pathology reading, suggesting that his family puts religious and cultural requirements before his education, whereas Aziz demonstrates agency in his resistance to this pressure. He was also the only boy who self-defined as Asian and he positively asserted a strong Asian masculinity in school at the same time as being well integrated in the school. He did not present as someone who was 'caught between cultures'.

Abid was a recognised high achiever in his school. He maintains that there that was no family pressure on him to put religion or culture before his academic work. Elsewhere (see chapter seven) he talked positively about strong maternal encouragement for his education which concurs with the research evidence on Asian women achievers (Ahmad, 2001; Abbas, 2004). Abid also checked to see if I was Muslim before answering a question in this first meeting. This is quite telling of his wider survivalist strategy in the school. He managed to perform a successful academic identity as well as being included within the dominant Asian peer group through strategic and 'safe' performances of 'bad boy' masculinity (see chapter seven). Sajid's account, like many of the other boys', revealed a social function of the mosque. It was not only a space for practising religion but a place for meeting friends when there was literally nothing else to do and nowhere to go.

Global politics

Because of the timing of the research, global politics emerged strongly as a theme across all the interviews. The boys strongly agreed that 9/11 and the ensuing 'war on terror' had had a significant impact on both school and community life. The following comments are typical of many expressed:

Arshad: ... like in their school there is a lot of racism because it's a Catholic school and because of Bin Laden and everything else yeah ... boom boom Bin Laden chuck a bomb in your back garden

FS: What do you mean 'because of Bin Laden'?

Arshad: Because Bin Laden chucked a bomb in their back garden

Malik: They all call me Bin Laden

FS: Do you get called Bin Laden?

Arif: Yeah everybody

Younis: You should call 'em Tony Bush [laughs] yeah Tony Bush [laughs]

            ***

            The thing is, they started thinking, since, ... like that incident happened, September 11th, they think all Muslims are terrorists when they haven't even got evidence that it was him [Bin Laden]. They're just accusing him because they're scared of him. (Arshad)

            ***

            They started being more sickening in their attitudes towards Asian people – they look at every other Asian as a terrorist ... they judge the whole crowd by ... they judge the majority by the minority. [Before 9/11] it was bad but not that bad. That just triggered it. They didn't used to call us terrorists then they used to call us Pakis. (Shahid)

            ***

            People are really sceptical about this whole thing, thinking there's justification for them to kill Muslims if they suspect that ... they can suspect what they want ... it's like a different day, a different era. And as much as the people have been discussing

61

9/11, it has had a massive impact on the community. We've had a lot of how can you put it ... from the white community ... Some really ignorant comments ... Like oh I wonder what it would be like 'you couldn't really go on holiday now could you?' Because we look like terrorists [to them]. ... That's the sort of stupid thing they're saying. Whatever they've been fed by the press that's what they've been repeating. Because they're white, they class themselves as being the same culture as the Europeans and the Americans. I don't see any belonging ... Growing up, Asian people have got this togetherness ... white people don't have in their own families let alone in their communities. (Yacoub, youth worker, Newtown)

***

Yeah cos if you go to read *namaz* in the mosque if you've got a beard people think Oh God, this is some Bin Laden person or he's like that, but everybody's not like that and we don't know if Bin Laden did that you know what I mean September 11 ... they haven't caught him yet. So it's getting much bad. We've had some really bad comments about Muslims but then I get really upset why are they saying that cos I'm a Muslim but I can't ... not everybody is like that And just people do talk about it cos like it's in the news too much isn't it? (Zahid)

***

As we used to walk home there's like many white people area we used to get called racist abuse like you terrorist and all this ... go back to Afghanistan and all this, and we aren't even from Afghanistan. (Hamid)

***

I was in year 7. No, beginning of year 8. I can remember the day actually ... it was a Tuesday. I've heard of stories like a woman and girl going to school in Birmingham and she had her *hijab* being ripped off. I've just heard stories. My cousin – his name's Osama. He goes to a school in London and everyone started to call him Osama Bin Laden. (Abid)

A number of themes emerge from these and other accounts of the impact of 9/11 on schooling:

First, at the local level of school and their local environments, the boys reported a significant increase in anti-Muslim racism, whether experienced through name calling, dissociation, discrimination or physical attack. However, the boys suggested that the events of September 11 and the ensuing 'war on terror' had not provoked any significant new experience – rather it had aggravated and intensified existing tensions and re-racialised them. As Shahid's account suggests, before 9/11 'it was bad, but not that bad'. The main new factor was the intensity of name-calling. Whereas in the past, boys had routinely been called 'Paki', the boys reported that terms such as *Afghani, terrorist,* and *suicide bomber* had been added to the general repertoire of racist insults. In addition to name-calling, the boys expressed an increased sense of stigmatisation because of being judged to be associated with Islamic terrorism.

A second theme to emerge from these accounts is the construction of polarised 'us and them' identities. That is, the boys drew specifically on *Muslim* 'we' identities which were constructed in relation to a collective 'they' composed of 'whites', 'Europeans' and 'Americans' sometimes collapsed into a single entity and at other times referenced interchangeably. Collectively 'they' at one level, were imbued with the power to judge Muslims in collusion with a powerful and highly partial media that also represented imperial interests. However, drawing on notions of community and family, the boys subverted these dominant readings by suggesting that Muslim and Asian family forms were stronger and less individualistic than white English forms, reversing cultural pathology argument. Yacoub uses it after recounting a catalogue of direct and indirect abuse that had been thrown at him recently. Zahid also made reference to differentiated forms of family, reversing cultural pathology arguments to suggest that white/English/European family forms lack the solidarity of Muslim and Asian family forms:

> To mix in with the English you need to be very different, like in our culture we don't move from our parents' house until we're married and we've got kids of our own, but they move out when they're eighteen. But then we're not like that because we respect out parents much more than these people. We take care of them. English parents are always in the [care] homes and you never see an Asian Pakistani or an Indian, everybody, just like their parents live with them. (Zahid)

Interestingly, in Zahid's account, superior family and cultural forms are inclusive of Indians. Elsewhere, however, (see chapter six) some boys went to great lengths to distinguish Pakistani Muslims from Indians.

The boys globalised their local predicaments through the association with a global Muslim brotherhood and distanced themselves from whites, who were constructed through discourses of family and community to be inferior and weak. They lack the 'togetherness' that Asian families own (Yacoub), and they 'don't look after their own' (Zahid). Archer (2003) found the boys in her study also constructed themselves and their family norms as superior to western and white family forms and cultural practices.

Thirdly, as in young people's recounts of the Paris Banlieues disturbances in 2005 (Cesari, 2007), scathing references were made to the role of the media in the perpetuation of racist discourses about Muslims and in the engineering of moral panics about Muslims. The DCLG (2009b) also found that most Muslim communities in Britain share this perception of the media as 'anti-Muslim'. The boys in my study constructed an all-powerful media as partial and strongly aligned to American, British and European imperial interests. This reading of imperialist media practice was also mediated by their local experiences of media in Oldwych which often reported stories about Muslims in negative and sensationalised ways. Stories often began with sentences such as, 'here we go again, Muslims have managed to...' suggesting that Muslims received favouritism from the local council or even that they were attempting to impose sharia law in the local area.

> You know that's the media, they twist everything ... it's always the white people who turn out to be good guys. Like in the films the Asians and that are always the bad. Whether it's Asian black, Chinese, they're still like that. It's always the Americans that are good. (Asad)
>
> ***
>
> Media is bad news. You know because at the end of the day who's running the media? Americans and all the British and they're the ones that hate Muslims. And at the end of the day, Muslims are going to take over one time and they ain't gonna like it. They'll come in numbers. (Arshad)
>
> ***

It was just like all everything was going bonkers basically. Like everyone was talking about it and taking the wrong idea because it was not the English people's fault it was the media's fault because they give the wrong idea to the public. (Zahid)

In these accounts we see strong observations that white people, mainly the working classes in their area, are the cultural dupes of the media: 'whatever they're fed by the press', Yacoub said earlier. And Zahid says he pities English people, implying that they lack the ability to distinguish propaganda from reality. Arshad invokes a 'clash of civilisations' (Huntingdon, 1997), suggesting that Muslims are hated by a West represented by Americans and the media and that Muslims will fight back. I would suggest that assertions of a strong Muslim identity represent a strategic response to counter and resist the widespread stigmatisation and anti-Muslim racism that the boys encountered through schooling and in their local environment post 9/11. These assertions helped to position the local white working class as weak and lacking in political literacy and therefore to subvert dominant discourses which positioned Muslims as, fundamentally, a threat to the Britishness of the nation.

Fourth, in virtually every interview the boys asserted that Bin Laden had been accused without evidence. They did not deny his guilt, nor did they paint him as a hero but rather as a victim of western conspiracy. Rather than this constituting support for Bin Laden and Islamic terrorism, the boys globalised their local predicaments. As we see in the next chapter, the boys felt they were disciplined more strongly by teachers than white students involved in similar incidents and, like Bin Laden were wrongly accused before the evidence was in. Abid for example, said, 'It was definitely wrong. They should have never done that. It was stupid. It could have been Tony Blair [who was responsible for 9/11]'. Aziz said, 'they say Bin Laden did it but they ... haven't got no proof. They haven't got no hard evidence. They just say it to spread round rumours that everyone believes it'. Saleem believes that Bin Laden is wrongly assumed to behind every act of terrorism:

It just got worse ... it's everywhere we go because every time some war kicks off on the TV or anything like that. Or any time a bomb goes off in any country, they think Bin Laden's behind it. Everything that goes on they think it's Muslims. (Saleem)

Whereas Osama Bin Laden was defended by boys because of his victim status, Saddam Hussein was overwhelmingly identified as an aggressor, as 'bad', 'greedy', 'he has golden toilets, while his people starve' (Rafiq) and as divisive:

> I don't really like him, to tell you the truth ... using missiles, he kills them and that's not right. Just because they're Shia. Why are you killing somebody for them that's wrong, and he says he's a Muslim and Shias are Muslim. I don't like him. (Aziz)

Although all the boys expressed dislike of Saddam, they pointed to a lack of evidence for weapons of mass destruction in Iraq and therefore questioned both the justification for the war and the US-British coalition's handling of it:

> No not like that ... if they wanted him they should just have gone in. Not bombed any city, not killed anybody, they should just have got him. They went in, bombed their place, destroyed everything, killed a lot of people and he's still in power ... He'll come back. They shouldn't even try to bomb the place until they find him. He's just one person ... they just wanted the oil. You distinguish people, Shias and other Muslims. Some people do that here. (Aziz)

> [Iraq's] even worse ... it's like you should just give Tony Blair, Saddam Hussain and George Bush each a gun and just tell 'em to fight their own battles and just kill themselves. (Abid)

Clearly, the boys were sceptical about the British and Americans, suggesting that their main motivation was material gain. Such comments challenge dominant views which position not only Muslims but young people in general as politically disengaged. As shown later in this chapter, the boys' accounts indicate strong engagements with local, national and global politics.

From 'Muslim' to 'Asian': the politics of cohesion and integration

Whereas the boys drew strategically on the notion of a global Muslim brotherhood in the discussion of global politics, they reverted to categorisations of Asian and Whites in relation to national level discourses of parallel lives, as discussed in chapter one. Aziz talks about David Blunkett's (then Labour Home Secretary) particularly proactive statements about Muslim Asian communities in the aftermath of 9/11 and the northern English town disturbances in 2001. As well as attacking practices such as arranged marriages, Blunkett suggested that such communities were insular.

Aziz: I just think he's just talking shit basically. Because actually when you look at Asians, they have white friends and some people do hate white people, they have real hatred for them. But we do have white friends. Some have a real hatred for white people that's what causes the trouble ... Me and all my mates hang out with white boys but if someone calls us Pakis then I don't get really offended, my mates get offended and stuff like that cos I'm like 'so what! You call me Paki but I'm from Britain', but my mates get offended

FS: Why do they get offended?

Aziz: They're Asian and they hate it when people call them Pakis ... some boys *are* from Pakistan and they don't get even get offended because they don't know what it means [laughs]

***

Asad: But that's our way of living. They've got to cope with it. We don't tell them to get married in a church so they shouldn't tell us ... I think every white person's a racist ...They won't show it but they are inside ... They say like look at that Asian there ... if they see more than two Asians they say look at them doing drugs ... causing trouble. That's what everybody thinks

Hamid: No Asians and whites do mix but there's like some who think there should be all white in England and no brown people like BNP pocket

FS: What do you say to those people?

Hamid: I hate 'em man

FS: You wouldn't talk to them?

Hamid: No they just want to beat me up

FS: What do you think is the solution, what do you think can be done to improve relations here?

***

FS: What's the best way to deal with racism?

Sajid: Just really get on with white people and make sure you're contributing. Get on with them and if they're not like good to you. If they're not contributing back you just leave them and go to the next person. That's what I've been doing and I've been getting on with them really well. They cause me no hassle

These Leyton boys' accounts show different strategies for dealing with local experiences. All challenge dominant discourses which present Muslim Asian communities as self-segregating. We saw earlier how the boys strategically took up Muslim identities to counter the widespread demonisation of Muslims. Here, however, we see a range of perspectives and identity positions on issues of integration. Aziz draws on a discourse of integration and belonging while at the same time challenging dominant discourses of parallel lives. He suggests that there is integration between different sections of working class communities around him. He recognises that there is common hatred in the deprived neighbourhood in which he lives and in the school, but that even so, people do mix. He claims that he is not easily provoked into fighting (though his teachers contested this). Aziz's response presents an integrationist perspective.

Asad, on the other hand, seems to confirm a discourse of self-segregation through his remark that every white person is a racist and that people should be able to live separately. However, his comments need to be read in the context of a recent incident in which he and his family were racially attacked physically, resulting in prosecution of the perpetrators. Mrs James told me that the school had been concerned about not only a drop in his academic progress but also about his social and personal welfare, as he had become withdrawn. His strong anti-white stance should be read as a shifted response in consequence of this incident.

Hamid presents an anti-racist strategy. As we will see, he was one of several boys actively involved in local and nationally organised anti-war protests. Sajid appears more integrationist but invokes a discourse of respect. Collectively the boys' responses present a clear assertion of strength and resilience and a discourse of mutual respect. They challenge dominant policy frameworks invoking both 'respect' and integration. For example, where these suggest one way traffic – working class youth are expected to *give* respect to other members of society but should not expect to receive it in return (Skeggs, 2004) – it is up to Asians to mix with white people, and not vice versa (Shain, 2010). The boys point out that cohesion requires the giving of respect on all levels and both sides.

Young people, politics and schooling

Recent policy and political debates have positioned young people, especially working class people, as politically alienated and apathetic. Through dominant discourses of respect, working class young people have been characterised as a disenchanted generation because of their apparent 'unwillingness to obey the law, to play by the rules, or to pay for the needs of others' (Mulgan and Wilkinson, 1997:218). Muslim youth have been positioned through dominant discourses of cohesion and the 'war on terror' as at risk of radicalisation and extremism.

The Crick report (1998), which provided the framework for the introduction of compulsory citizenship education in secondary schools in 2002, stated that political apathy among the young was 'inexcusably and damagingly bad'. It concluded that democracy was under threat and that the introduction of compulsory citizenship was necessary to help stem the rising tide of political disengagement among young people. Cunningham and Lavallette (2004) argue that the Crick report aimed 'at no less than a change in the political culture of this country both nationally and locally'. It urged young people to be encouraged 'to think of themselves as active citizens, willing, able and equipped to have an influence in public life [and to become] ... confident in finding new forms of involvement and action among themselves' (1998:7). However, as a number of commentators have argued, the model of political participation drawn on by the Crick report and subsequent citizenship education frameworks is based on too narrow a focus around domestic politics and on the rights and responsibilities of citizens (Osler, 2009; Gillborn, 2006). Bhavnani (1994) observed that young people are engaged in a range of political causes including anti-globalisation and third world debt, and evidence suggests that children and young people's participation in such movements has actually increased in recent years.

Cunningham and Lavallette (2004) note that the model of Citizenship Education instituted by New Labour at the same time as calling for more critical engagement in politics, also retains a social control function inherited from the previous Conservative government's model.

Introduced under the guise of 'cross-curricular themes', the Conservative model focused primarily on being a good citizen by 'helping others' – an aspect that seems to have resurfaced in David Cameron's notion of volunteering expressed during the 2010 national election campaign.

Davies (2001:307) points out the potential for confusion and contradiction within a curriculum that seeks 'on the one hand, to foster compliance, obedience, a socialisation into social norms and citizen duties; and on the other, to encourage autonomy, critical thinking and the citizen challenge to social injustice' is quite high. Cunningham and Lavellete found that in practice, many school students report that citizenship classes are reduced to a rehashing of moral questions about sex and drug-taking. Muslim youth, on the other hand, have been characterised through dominant discourses of radicalisation as vulnerable to the 'wrong sort' of politics, coded through the term 'political alienation' (Alexander, 2004) which places them 'at risk' of extremism.

Contrary to current political discourses, which position young people as disinterested and lacking knowledge about politics, the boys in this study demonstrated strong political awareness and can be regarded as 'competent social and political actors' (Hopkins, 2007; Cunningham and Lavallette, 2004; Skelton and Valentine, 2003). As we have seen, their strong opinions on global, national and local politics indicated an active engagement with political issues and they took up a range of strategies to counter dominant discourses on the 'war on terror', while also challenging discourses of segregation. Most notable was the discursive construction of a strong Muslim collectivity – or global Islamic brotherhood – to counter media and public discourses which positioned all Muslim as terrorists.

The boys' readiness to talk about politics across the interviews indicated active engagement rather than political alienation:

> Turkey's close to Iraq. It's next door. Turkish might join in. Iraq. Kurdish groups might attack Turkey now ... might try to take over. If Turkey has a war with America all the Muslim countries, Pakistan will join together. (Ibrahim)

***

> Wahid:　　There was something in the news the other day there was a British person who tried to save two Muslim people ... and the Israelis shot him.

Arif:	Was that Tom something? [Tom Hurndall]
Wahid:	Yeah that's it ... he's in a coma
Arif:	And the woman too [Rachel Corrie]
Wahid:	Yeah they rammed into her ...Three actually who died ... in the last 3-4 months. You don't hear much about it on the news
Arif:	No ... the odd story ... this happened
Wahid:	The media's always attacking Muslims ... when 9/11 happened it was on for about two months ... and then when they were attacking Afghanistan it was about a week in December

While discursively taking up global Muslim identities, some of the boys were also involved in local efforts which required alliances with non-Muslims to organise resistance to the wars in Afghanistan and Iraq. Hamid and two other boys (Sajid and Tariq) had attended both the 28 September 2002 demonstration against the prospect of war on Afghanistan and the historic demonstration against the war on Iraq on 15 February 2003 in London, organised by the Stop the War Coalition. The boys talked about other people they knew had been at the demonstrations in Birmingham and about a thwarted attempt at Greenbank school to organise a day of protests in early March 2003 in line with other school strikes that took place across Europe at that time. The demonstrations against the prospect of war on Iraq provided the context for a series of school based protests towards the end of February in Europe and on the eve of the war in March 2003. Pupils in several schools walked out of classes and gathered in town and city centres, calling for 'peace not war'. This was described as a new kind of protest and – most significantly, child-led – campaign for a century. Children as young as ten were reported to have walked out of classes (Cunningham and Lavallete, 2004).

The boys reported that attempts to organise a day of protests at nearby Greenbank school had been met with a lock-down. At Leyton, support for the protests had not been as strong as in Greenbank but Hamid reported that he and his friends – Muslim and non-Muslim – had been prepared to act together. Such accounts challenge both dominant discourses of apathy among young people and discourses of segregation.

71

Hamid:	There was going to be one in Greenbank but teachers called the police down ... We were going to have one here but the teachers heard about it and it was stopped
FS:	Would that have been Muslims or mixed?
Hamid:	It would have been mixed, to tell the truth right, a lot of my friends they were saying that yeah ... but they just wanted to for the fun of it get out of school

Hamid defines his friends' motivation for getting involved as truancy and this was to become the official education establishment response (Woodhead, 2003): that young people were motivated by irresponsible truancy rather than genuine political activism. Hamid does say that his friends were keen to be involved because of the prospect of missing school, but elsewhere the boys reported a more concerted and organised network of activities that challenges the idea that truancy was the primary motivating factor in the school protests.

> Just walked out of the school ... yeah I heard about that someone texted me but that was mostly people ... there's only about 50 odd people in the whole, and they couldn't really do much about it and plus it was also holidays when that happened. I was home when I heard about it. (Zahid)

Zahid was not tempted to join in, perhaps because he was keen to stay on the right path for the sake of his academic achievement. Wahid said he had been prepared to be involved but criticised others in his school for not caring enough about the issues: 'they just don't care' (Wahid).

As Cunningham and Lavellete (2004:257) have argued:

> The contradiction at the heart of citizenship education has been revealed by the attitude of both schools and the educational establishment to young people's actions against the war on Iraq. While some heads and teachers supported children's right to protest, the dominant view of the educational establishment was that the strikes represented an 'unruly' excuse to truant.

Hamid, Sajid, Wasim and another friend had taken part in the national demonstrations. Here Hamid talks about his involvement in the London demonstration on 15 February:

Hamid:	Yeah I went to one in London
FS:	Can you tell me a bit about that? What was it like?
Hamid:	Alright there was like enough people. I went on a bus like a few

	people from Newtown went on a bus but I felt tired, had to walk for a long time ... hungry an all. The shops were packed out couldn't get much
FS:	When was that?
Hamid:	It was about 5 months ago
FS:	February 15 ? The big massive one, the 2 million one?
Hamid:	Yeah. Miss Dynamite!
FS:	Did you get into Hyde Park?
Hamid:	Yeah
FS:	What made you want to go on that demonstration?
Hamid:	I just wanted to go see what it was like cos I'd been to one before when Afghanistan happened in London and I wanted to go again
FS:	How was it organised?
Hamid:	Oh erm from the Newtown mosque some people came there – don't know who they were and they put a poster up that a coach is leaving from here to thingy so I went from there. I saw the notice and decided to go.
FS:	Would you go again?
Hamid:	Yeah

Such conversations challenge not only the dominant educational esta-blishment view that young people are politically alienated and a short walk from extremism, but also the tabloid response to the school based protests that suggested they were exclusively engaged in and orches-trated by white middle class students. The boys' discussions revealed a strong engagement with class politics that defy these assumptions. Virtually all of them readily engaged in discussions of global and national politics, all reported watching news, often reluctantly with their parents, and all were able to engage in local, national and global political discussions.

Teaching and 'war on terror'

It was clear from the boys' accounts that home was a bigger factor than school in their political socialisation. One of the frustrations expressed by the boys was the lack of open, informed and critical discussion in school about the 'war on terror'. Discussion about 9/11 and the 'war on terror' left many of the boys feeling further marginalised. Asad, for example, mentioned an attempt to discuss the issue in school assemblies. This was usually arranged in the context of rising tensions nationally or when a fight had broken out, usually in response to tensions in school. Ibrahim observed that, 'In English we do war as part of our syllabus, but there hasn't be anything on Iraq'. Asad remarked that teachers only talked about it in assemblies:

> They did every now and then in assemblies but they always made Iraq out to be the bad side and straight away pointed to Osama Bin Laden. They haven't got no proof he did it they got all these tapes but they could have been made up. Anyway, the CIA intelligence could have done anything so you don't know who's telling the truth these days. (Asad)
>
> - - -

Asad: We're always made out to be the bad guys...

FS: By who?

Asad: Everybody ... the white people. The teachers you know they're you know they always take the side of white people ... and they'll try to make us out to be wrong, saying Saddam Hussein killed his own people and he did this he did that

FS: Are there many teachers who are sympathetic, understand ...?

Asad: Yeah there are most of 'em are sympathetic anyway but they still think Saddam's in the bad and George Bush is in the right

FS: Do they actually say that?

Asad: They don't say it but they say it in a certain way. They imply it ... cos in this school everything's crafty

FS: Crafty?

Asad: They say it in a certain way ... they know what they're trying to say but they won't say it ...

As we see from Asad's account, teachers are perceived to be sympathetic on an individual level but Asad felt that in the institutionalised mediation of the 'war on terror' the dominant version of the truth was too readily reproduced. He suggested that teachers were careful not to verbally take sides but the lack of critical discussion meant that the dominant media and political version was left unchallenged.

Although Asad said that there was no explicit discussion of the 'war on terror', Hamid reported a spontaneous attempt to tackle the issue in a history lesson:

> Some of the history teachers talk about now yeah saying asking me and this other Asian in the class, yeah ... he goes 'what are you going to do after you leave school?' Yeah, and the other Asian friend, for a joke said 'we'll join the Taliban' and then we had a whole lesson, instead of doing work, yeah, we were talking about 'why do young Asian men want to join the Taliban?'

FS: What kind of things were you saying?

Hamid: We were saying that er Muslims say, that all Muslims should stick up for each other and stuff like that

FS: Do you believe that ... would you?

Hamid: Kind of yeah ... I wouldn't actually go to war and that ... I don't want to get killed ... but if my own friends have a fight then I would

Again we see the globalising of local predicaments. Although he draws on the analogy of war, and initially claims that he would join the Taliban, Hamid is quite clear that he should not actually go war to defend a common Muslim brotherhood. He would, though, stand up for his friends and defend them should the need arise. Asad's and Hamid's accounts indicate that certain teachers were constructed by the boys as 'sympathetic' and understanding. Some were also reported to be willing to abandon prepared lesson plans to discuss the impact of the 'war on terror' on the schooling and local environments. Schooling as a formal institution, however, was constructed by the boys to be ineffective in formally challenging the Islamophobia embedded in dominant discourses of the 'war on terror'.

Conclusion

This chapter has discussed issues of identity in relation to politics and religion, and how the discourses of the 'war on terror' were being mediated in the context of schooling. Contrary to current political discourses which position young people as disinterested and ignorant about politics, the boys in this study showed strong political awareness and in some cases activism that suggest they should be regarded as 'competent social and political actors' (Skelton and Valentine, 2003; Cunningham and Lavallette, 2004; Hopkins, 2007), rather than disaffected or disengaged. The strong opinions the boys expressed about global, national and local politics indicated their active engagement with political issues.

The boys adopted a range of strategies to counter dominant discourses on the 'war on terror' that position Muslims as the problem. Some countered dominant discourses through the assertion of strong collective Muslim families which were discursively constructed as superior to the individualistic western, European, white norms and family practices. Some made provocative statements that seemed to buy into the new-found notoriety as Muslim radicals, while others talked about engagement in national anti-war protests and local school-based protests. Collective Muslim identities were built on self definitions as Muslim first, but this was not a fixed identity. The next chapter looks at the construction of an alternative masculinity that was constructed in opposition to what was perceived as the white racist and imperialist culture of the school.

4

'Asian boys run the school': racism and peer relations

Introduction

The last chapter explored the construction of a collective Muslim identity as a strategic response to the racialised and stigmatised status of being a Muslim in school. Collective Muslim identities were built on self-definitions as 'Muslim first'. This was not, however, a fixed identity and this chapter considers an alternative 'Asian' identity that was constructed by the boys in opposition to the dominant relations of schooling which were constructed as white and racist. The chapter focuses on the peer group as the centrepiece for the construction of racialised masculine identities in the context of schooling.

Ethnographic studies of schooling have documented a range of cultures and subcultures that are played out and contested in the context of informal learning. These cultures and subcultures have been identified in research to be constructed in relation to dominant institutionalised definitions of 'success' and 'failure'. Willis's (1977) 'lads' rejected the formal curriculum of the school and constructed as feminine a group of academically orientated students whom they labelled 'earoles'. Connells's (1989) 'swots', 'cool boys' and 'wimps', Mac an Ghaill's (1994) 'academic achievers' and 'macho lads', Kessler *et al*'s (1985) sporting 'bloods' and academic 'Cyrils' all represent oppositional subcultures where success is feminised and against which alternative successful masculine identities are developed (Renold, 2005).

The boys in my study reported similar divisions and differences in academic orientations to schooling, with the main marker the difference between 'snobs' and 'normal' people. However, these academically located divisions were also cross-cut by gender and ethnicity and in particular a dominant racialised division between Asian and white boys. 'Clever' high achieving Asian boys – who were in a minority – were labelled as 'snobs' while simultaneously acquiring social status through their friendships with a dominant group of 'tough' Asian boys.

Friends

When asked to name their friends, most of the boys mentioned other Asian boys in their school first. In Leyton School, the boys most commonly cited were Aziz, Sajid, Tariq, Toyab, Wasim and Sadiq. Aziz was the 'dominant popular' (Willis, 2003) boy and featured at the top of virtually every list. Sajid, Tariq, Toyab, Wasim and Sadiq were named as runners up. Other mainly Pakistani and Bangladeshi boys featured on the outskirts of the group and the Asian boys' peer group also included of Afghani and Turkish boys, who formed a minority in the schools. As the comments below illustrate, these boys were adopted as part of the group and also identified with them.

Farood:	They call me 'Afghani' or 'Paki'
FS:	What do you say when they say 'Afghani'?
Farood:	I beat them up
FS:	When the first time someone called you 'Paki' what did you think?
Farood:	When someone called me 'Paki', I said why you calling me 'Paki'? They should be called Pakistani
FS:	Did you know what it meant?
Farood:	No
FS:	You didn't know why they were saying it?
Farood:	Yeah ... I said why did you call them 'Paki'? They said because they are here and they have everything and they fight with us ... it's my country ... it's not your business
FS:	Do other boys get called 'Paki'?
Farood:	No ... They're scared ... because if they call us 'Paki', we beat 'em up

* * *

Tariq talking about Farood:

Tariq:	But we like to say he's Pakistani ... like us, because none of us are like, different. We're all the same ... no-one's an outcast.
FS:	Who?
Tariq:	All of us Asians
FS:	What about the white boys?
Tariq:	Well some whites are ok with us ... some cause problems but ... not any more now. It's all sorted now

***

Ibrahim:	I just hang out with all the Asian boys
FS:	And how is that?
Ibrahim:	Like, they don't see me as different cos I'm like Turkish or anything

The first extract shows how Farood initially positions himself as simultaneously within and outside the boundaries of 'Pakistani'. At first he says he doesn't know why *they* are called Pakis. However, when he speaks about being strong and fighting back, he positions himself within this category: 'we beat them up'. In the second extract, Tariq constructs Farood as being part of the group by virtue of his similarities with Pakistanis. Ibrahim's account also confirms that he is included as part of the group. This inclusion of Other Muslims was possible at Leyton because of their extremely small numbers, for example there were two Turkish boys in the school, one of whom had recently left, and three Afghani boys. In London, where the majority of the Turkish community reside, there are reported rivalries between larger group of Turkish boys and Pakistanis and Bangladeshis. In other areas, such as the north west of England, Pakistani and Bangladeshi boys are also reported to be engaged in fierce struggles over ethnic differences and identities.

'Safe' white boys and 'John boys'

Contrary to dominant policy and public discourses of segregation (Cantle, 2001), a significant number of white boys were also cited by the boys as friends, although white boys were never 'best' friends but part of a secondary list. White boys were more likely to be cited as friends in individual interviews, where the boys displayed 'softer versions of mas-culinity' (Frosch *et al*, 2002) than in the paired and group interviews where 'race' talk provided a source of bonding among Asian group members (*ibid*; Archer, 2003). Across the individual interviews 'safe', 'cool' and 'sound' white boys were distinguished from 'racist, 'bad' 'trouble-makers' who were commonly identified as the instigators of racialised fighting.

Thus the peer group was more loosely and flexibly structured than in traditional accounts of working class school subcultures (Willis, 1977; Corrigan, 1976) and some white boys were included as 'honorary' Asian boys. A number of the boys also mentioned white girls as part of their friendship group and this, as I discuss in this chapter and the next, was a further source of tension between the two dominant groups of 'tough boys' at the schools. In group but not individual interviews, white boys were often referred to as 'John boys' and this appeared to be part of the bonding process between groups of boys:

Yasser:	In the toilets it says 'Bin Laden is a non-Muslim'
Arshad:	... so he rubbed it off [laughs]
Yasser:	[laughs]
Mushtaq:	Who do you think written that? Umar or ...
Yasser:	No, some 'John boy'
FS:	Why do you call them 'John boys'?
Arshad:	They call us *Chacha* [uncle] man so we call 'em 'John boys'
Yasser:	John's name – you say 'what's your name?' [they say], 'JOHN' [laughs]
Muddasser:	Yeah. John or Dave!
Saleem:	..... a *Gora* is white person ...
Arshad:	...they [referring to interviewers] know what a *Gora* is ...
Saleem:	*Gora, gora* looks like a *pakora* [laughs]
Yasser:	Gora's snog *attah*

Attah is the flour used to make chappatis and pakora an onion bhaji. *Gora* (white) is now a commonly applied term of abuse but lacks the racially charged power of 'Paki'. Nonetheless it is commonly applied in a form of reverse-racism that has been said by some to produce feelings of injustice among white boys and a sense of white defensiveness (Gill-born, 1996). The labels of 'John boy' and 'Chacha man' also suggest an element of mutual recognition in the boys' banter and they too were less racially charged than 'Paki' or 'terrorist' or 'honkey'.

'Really religious' boys and Asian masculinity

Boys who were positioned and who also positioned themselves as religiously Muslim (the 'really religious' boys) were also included in the Asian boys' group, which demonstrates their multiple identity positionings. Zahid and Rafiq actively dissociated from activities engaged in by the Asian boys, most notably smoking and mixing with white girls. For Rafiq it was specifically romantic relations with white girls that represented the main dividing line between his take up of Asian identity and that of the 'tough' Asian boys. Because they did not fully participate in such activities, Zahid and Rafiq were located on the outskirts of, but still within, the friendship group. Umar, another of the 'really religious' boys, however, seemed to penetrate the inner core of the Asian boys' group more easily than the other 'religious' boys, despite taking issue with their relationships with white girls – possibly because he also hung out with the boys out of school.

Racism, stigma and the construction of Asian masculinities

As Alexander (2000) argues: 'a crucial element in the creation and maintenance of peer group boundaries is their oppositional nature'. In Alexander's study, this was manifested in two distinct but connected ways. The first was 'the imposition of a collective, usually stigmatised, identity from outside' and the second 'through the formulation of notions of inclusion and exclusion from the young men themselves'. For the young men in Alexander's study, the 'boundaries of friendship were formulated and sustained in the interstices of stigma and danger, and though not fully contained within these parameters, group identity was crucially built on a sense of collective defiance under fire' (2000: 157-8). The Asian boys' friendship group was similarly constructed externally and internally through a sense of 'collective defiance under fire'.

Racism

The majority of the boys who were positioned and positioned themselves as part of an all-Asian male peer group were in the lower sets at school. However, the group's identity went beyond sets and was in this sense racialised. Racism was cited as a defining and central aspect of the boys' experiences of school and was a significant external factor in the construction of the Asian male peer group. However, as the boys' comments reveal, racism took different shapes and forms, ranging from the mundane but deeply ingrained level of name-calling to institutionalised disciplinary mechanisms through which the Asian boys were constructed as problems. The all-Asian male peer group was therefore externally constructed by a collective sense of stigmatisation. The boys talked about being labelled interchangeably as gang members, trouble makers, and sometimes they were stigmatised simply as 'Muslims'.

Mushtaq: My school's very racist, the teachers are racist ... [they] don't like Asians

Mudasser: If an Asian has a fight with a gora, they think it's a racial fight straight away – even though it might be over something else. They'll say it's racist and they'll treat it differently and the thing is yeah, there was one Jamaican teacher who stuck up for me in that school – apart from that none stuck up for me except for me and my mates

***

Arshad: There was a kerfuffle and someone hit this guy on the head with a dotty hammer, no names like everyone knows who he is and he hit this guy in the head with a dotty hammer and the other guy slashed him in the head with the scissors and with a pen – this is *gora* and this is five minutes before – there was no ... Every day there's a teacher in the canteen; that day there wasn't and there was already trouble in the school and it just kicked off in the canteen then they went down the corridor and Mudasser over there, hit a guy with a dotty hammer ... We found out afterwards that some guy had crushed his fingers and they had to call Aziz Khan in and the thing was yeah that they wouldn't treat us ... and we called Aziz Khan and Dev Patel from the REC – and as soon as ... [they] turn up they treat us differently but then when Aziz went they treat us differently again. Like once Aziz came in ... as soon as he's walking out this kid shouted racial abuse at Aziz and when he'd walked in the classroom and like, the teachers were dealing with it and they asked the head teacher to go for the equal opportunities policy and they, oh God, they starting panicking...

Mushtaq: ... this kid, he's in Wasim 's class ... Aziz walked past and he went ' bud, bud' like that, do you get me?

***

Zahid: It's a very good school. Teachers are nice and most of the students are ok too. Some member of staff and some of the student could be racist who could make racist comments but they don't really make them to your face, they do it to your back ...

While Zahid, a relatively high achiever, speaks of covert racism, the previous extract suggests that the others defined the experience of schooling in relation also to institutionalised and sometimes violent racism. Through these and other accounts, the boys painted a picture of their schools as institutionally racist. The first account suggests that any fight involving Asians and white boys is immediately racialised by staff. In the second extract, Arshad implies that lip service was paid to equal opportunities. He suggests that teachers performed in line with race equality when under scrutiny but switched back to routine racialised performances once they were beyond the gaze of the Racial Equality Council. Further, he suggests that teachers lacked authority and control and consequently students felt unsafe and unsupported. Importantly, however, at other times, the same students mentioned how quickly the teachers intervened in fights. In one case, a teacher had his glasses broken while trying to prise apart two warring boys. There were other references to teachers 'flying out of nowhere' to stop a fight. But the collective accounts of racialised exclusion overshadowed these individualised instances and were central to the formation of an all-Asian male friendship group.

Disciplinary techniques: the institutionalisation of the Asian gang
The sense of stigma was shared right across the sets and by both Muslim and other Asian boys, helping to create a strong Asian identity. Abid, the highest achieving Asian boy at Leyton, commented on the labelling of Asian boys as gang members:

Abid:	They say like ... all the people think there's a gang of Asians and they're just friends and one of the English boys who's with us, he's getting abuse off a boy and this guy in the top group he's saying to this [other] guy 'stop it' and he's saying 'oh, what you going to do? Going to get your gang of Asian boys onto me...?'
FS:	Really?
Abid:	The teachers even think that ... they saying , oh er, like before a few months ago we were allowed, there's this classroom there and we were allowed to sit, well not sit, but stand [outside it] but now it seems that teachers are moving us away from there
FS:	Why do you think Asian lads are being moved on?
Abid:	Because they're said to cause most of the trouble
FS:	And are there Asian gangs?
Abid:	No not really

***

Arif:	Teachers take the white people side more
Wahid:	Cos like they don't split them up. They let them be in their gangs ... they always split us up so that only one or two of us ...
FS:	Why do you think that happens?
Wahid:	Cos they favour the white people ... it obvious isn't it?

Abid's account reveals that the perceived status as stigmatised was a significant factor in the construction of the Asian boys' group at Leyton. White boys who hang around with Asian boys are racialised as supplementary Asian gang members but constructed as weak through their apparent need of gang protection. This construction reinforces the toughness of the Asian boys. The Newtown boys painted a similar picture of being labelled by teachers and students as gang members in their schools, suggesting that the dominant stereotype of Asian gangs was an institutionalised aspect of their schooling.

The group's identity was further confirmed by the disciplinary techniques employed by teachers, in particular the practice of separating and moving groups of boys. The boys claimed to be disciplined more harshly as a result of being perceived as part of a gang.

School ... they've been alright ... well ... I don't approve of what they did. It's like almost every year we have a racist gang war in this school and it's almost every year or every two to three years, where all the Asians come together and get suspended. They'll suspend the Asians for nine weeks and the white people who caused it, they'll get suspended for one or two weeks. We just don't get that and if we complain then there'll be more trouble after that. (Asad)

Asad's perceptions are supported by Ofsted's confirmation that there were a disproportionate number of fixed-term exclusions of Muslim boys. To take just one statistic, sixteen fixed-term exclusions were of Bengali boys, of whom there were only fourteen in the entire school.

Another factor in the collective sense of stigmatisation felt by group members had to do with being a Muslim. This meant that boys who were not Asian but who defined themselves as Muslim could be included in the group. As Zahid observes, Muslim students were judged against a dominant narrative of Muslims as threatening and dangerous and as ultimate Others.

Zahid: It was just like all everything was going bonkers basically. Like everyone was talking about it and taking the wrong idea because it was not the English people's fault it was the media's fault because they give the wrong idea to the public and everything was going on about Muslims going on then and I didn't really like it. I didn't like coming into school them days because of the amount of people who were just talking about Muslims that they're like this and like that

FS: Yeah ... so what kind of things were they saying about Muslims?

Zahid: Right only cos if you were a Muslim that all Muslims are like that? You could realise they weren't talking about individual Muslims but then you could realise that they were talking about us at the same time

Reputation, respect and the maintenance of peer group boundaries

Rafiq talking about Aziz:

Well sometimes ... one of our friends. He's new. And he was walking home on his own down there after the gate. Loads of them started calling him 'Paki' and he came home and one of us from Newtown went back then and there was fighting. Last year was probably the biggest fights all of year 9,10 and 11 *goray* ... Rough them lot are. Outside in the field ... one's happening by the ash one's happening by the fields here ... one's happening up there ... the teachers won't have enough places to go ... terrible

FS: So what normally happens?

Rafiq: What normally we just normally go help out but sometimes if they get caught on their own then we don't know what happens say, if we get jumped by two people. [We] ... might win, might not ... well I know he'll win straight way ... I've seen him do it. He's fast

FS: So he's fast?

Rafiq: He's *rough* (admiringly). Don't mess with him. Farood' s ok too. He's pretty hard he is ... pushed me he has

FS: You said you all get on and look after each other

Rafiq: No there's like a little jab yeah ... but bang he hurt me proper ... but he hasn't had a fight in school yet. Unlike the other one ... Rahim ... he has fights and gets battered most of the time

FS: Why?

Rafiq: I don't know how his fight's start. He just thinks he's number one

FS: Is that important to be number one?

Rafiq: No not really cos all you come into school for is education not fighting is it?

FS: But there seems to be a lot of fighting

Rafiq: Yeah but in year 7, 8 and 9 I thought yeah ok but now year 10 and 11 we've got to concentrate now ... GCSEs are coming up

***

Farood: They [white boys] say to Rahim 'what you are going to do [are you] – going to get your gang of Asians on to us?' He got battered again the other day

Internally, the peer group was hierarchically structured, although loosely, in terms of membership. Aziz was widely recognised as the 'real number one' but this positioning was contested on a daily basis, including by subordinated internal members such as Rahim. An ideal Asian masculinity was embodied in Aziz, who was collectively identified by the core of the Asian boys' group at Leyton as the 'toughest' boy in the Asian boys' peer group. As Rafiq describes, Aziz embodied strength and speed and he was 'not to be messed with'. He had proven credentials as a tough fighter. This recognised status as the toughest Asian boy was one of the reasons Aziz was identified as being targeted for attack by white boys. Thus, within the Asian peer group and across peer groups there was a constant 'jostling for position' (Kessler *et al*, 2005).

As we see from Rafiq's account, Rahim, although already a fighter, is positioned relationally as weak. He did not know when to fight and when to leave well alone. Play fighting served an important function and was a way for the boys to try out their strength in the safety of the group but at the same time it was a bid for status and position. Through play fighting, Farood took Rafiq by surprise and at the same time earned respect and status as a real contender for the inner core of the Asian boys' group. In both accounts, Rahim is positioned relationally as weak. This concurs with findings of studies showing how masculinities are relationally produced, contested and negotiated on a daily basis (Connell, 1985, 2005; Swain, 2001, 2002; Renold, 2005).

Rafiq's account also suggests that it is impossible to perform valued social *and* academic identities (Youdell, 2004). As discussed in chapter seven, several boys talked about 'leaving tough boy masculinities' (Archer and Yamashita, 2002) in year 11 so they could concentrate on their work.

Other resources drawn on in the internal construction of the Asian boys' peer group included: loyalty, sticking up for mates and being smart, all evident in research studies of hegemonic masculinity (Martino, 1999; Skelton, 2001; Swain, 2001; Renold, 2005). Fighting and football were dominant tools in the bid for successful tough boy masculinities.

Aziz: That's why when there are fights they call their friends around cos they live local they get their friends over. Cos it's mainly a white area. Basically if I walk on the street now I'll most likely get jumped or I get swore at, ' Paki' ... When they say 'Paki' I don't really get bothered. I just say you're white

FS: They jump you physically?

Aziz:	Yeah ... Just walking on that road
Aziz:	If I walk on that road there, there's young lads they start staring at me and if I look back, whatever, they'll start following and if there's a road that's empty they'll either try to jump me or chase me
FS:	And you have to walk there every day?
Aziz:	No I just come up the bottom
FS:	And do they come that way?
Aziz:	Couple of times they've come from the top ... they jump us, but we run away (smiling) cos we're faster ... and three of the boys in year 11 they've got cars

***

FS:	How did you get this reputation for helping each other?
Tariq:	Just happened. We just say that ok if one of us has a fight I'm going to jump in so it will always kick off ... that's what Aziz says. He's the hardest one here ... Saleem ... do you know Saleem?
FS:	Yeah
Tariq:	He's supposed to have a fight down there by the bus stop and if anyone else jumps in then he's [Aziz] said he's definitely going to join in as well ...
FS:	And do they join in or do they just say that?
Tariq:	They do! Cos once his brother Rizwan he's in a higher college. Even though he's younger. He had a fight with the college people, he [Aziz] don't care ...

These accounts show why Aziz occupies the position of top dog among the Asian boys: he is smarter, faster, tougher and also willing to stand up for others.

The collective talk of backup and helping out others invokes notions of community ethos (Alexander, 2000). Elsewhere this was reinforced by the equation of white culture with individualism and Asian culture as collective and strong (see also Archer, 2003). As we see in chapters five and seven, this strong collective identity and sense of community challenge dominant accounts of individualisation that suggest the influence of social structures of class, race and gender in young people's lives is declining. We see complex intersections of local and historical cultures, both in a residual activist Asian culture from the 1980s documented in Ramamurthy (2006) and local working class communities.

Settlements

In the interviews, the boys inferred that Asian boys had in the past 'run' the school (Alexander, 2000; Archer, 2003) but now, because of their numerical inferiority in the school, white boys felt able to challenge the physical dominance of the Asian boys:

> Because before, yeah, like there used to be quite a few Asian who used to come to this school and it was mainly like you know 'run' by Asians. Now that there's hardly any Asians yeah like all the white kids start like fighting, start being racist and that so like there's quite a few fights. (Hamid)
>
> ***
>
> Normally they're scared. But because we're the oldest and we've got exams and stuff like that they thought they could retaliate. (Asad)
>
> ***
>
> My cousin Murad was here ... that's when their fights happened ... when we came [the white boys] started on us but just before they [the Asian boys] left they sorted everything out so if anything happens we help our Asians. If one is against one lad, all of us come in. That's why they don't say nothing now. All of us jump in so that's why nobody dare say nothing now ... they're scared. (Tariq)
>
> ***
>
> They're all scared of us. They just stay away every time we walk past the corridors they just get out of the way ... even one of us ... because they know if even one of us gets thumped out on the corridor the other ones just come running up ... out of nowhere. They just know something is happening. (Rahim)
>
> ***

Aziz:	They cause the trouble, year 7 do ... They get a bit hyperactive and kick off and expect us to jump in. Sometimes we hit em but then we think why I'm a hitting a year 7?
FS:	Why do they start acting like that?

Aziz: When we get into trouble like they think they're fighting that they get a big reputation. People get scared of you and they [year 7s] get hyper

FS: And do you get a big reputation?

Aziz: No not really just get a bad reputation with the teachers

FS: What about from people around you?

Aziz: Around me? like all these are my friends ... year 11s a few lads are scared of me they know I'll flip on them. I've got a reputation

Thus there appears to be a constant battle for position between the dominant Asian and white peer groups and a 'brotherhood' among Asian students. Older boys would endeavour to leave the school on having established their position as superior fighters. Younger boys would then draw on their apprenticeship within the safety net of the older boys' network, to fight their own battles for top position. Group solidarity was central to maintaining the hegemony of the Asian boys' group. This talk of settlements constructed white boys as opportunistic and sly, reversing colonial stereotypes of Muslims as sly and untrustworthy. White boys waited for opportune moments, for example, when the established regime was temporarily distracted through exams, or a local trip to the mosque, to make their bid for power: 'Every now and then, the [white boys] try it on, but we beat em down' (Riaz, Newtown).

Aziz's account shows that he is acutely aware that the reputation within the group does not transfer to respect from the teachers. Social reputation was paramount for Aziz and he invested heavily in fostering it at the expense of an academic reputation.

Linguistic code switching

If the labelling of white boys as 'John boy' did not subordinate white boys, linguistic code switching was employed (Qureshi, 2004). The boys switched between English and Punjabi or Bengali as another way of maintaining peer group boundaries. Turkish and Afghani boys were temporarily marginalised by such linguistic exclusion aimed at white boys and teachers. The comments below show that some white boys now recognised the most common expletives and knew when they were being abused. The Asian boys most commonly justified their use of their home languages as being because they needed privacy. White students and teachers, however, were aware of the power of exclusion of this mechanism.

Asad:	No specific situations ... just a bit of privacy from these lot
Hamid:	Like when the teachers there and they trying to know what you're saying but you
Sajid:	When we're outside we just talk in our own language
FS:	Any reason?
Sajid:	No we just do it. It just comes out [laughs]
FS:	What if English people say we don't know what you're saying? How do you respond?
Sajid:	...... they've never said that to us ... because when we're all in bunch we just start talking and when we're bored in lessons we just talk and they just like 'What? What?'
FS:	Haven't they picked up any words yet?
Sajid:	No they say it again. Some of em – *goray* – know a few swear words now and again, they're always learning to talk of us when we swear. They just pick it up.
Hamid:	We just like to tie it off in our language

Here we see Hamid and Sajid, who had claimed to have strong friendships with white boys and girls, performing an exclusionary identity through linguistic switching. As Sajid says, such mechanisms were often used in lessons to defeat boredom or when they found work difficult. However, their battles with boredom in the classroom and with 'racist' or 'bad' white boys at times outweighed the need to have white friends.

Football and racialised fight-talk

Sporting affiliations are significant markers of race and nation (see chapter five). Football was the main sport through which hegemonic masculinities are constructed. Empirical studies (Renold, 1997; 2005, Connolly, 1998; Skelton, 2000; Swain, 2001; Nayak, 2003) have sought to investigate the role of football as a key signifier in constructing hegemonic masculinities in school. Connell (2005:15) argues that:

[while] organised competitive team sport, a distinctly modern social practice, is intensely gender segregated and male dominated, sports such as football are also extraordinarily popular with high rates of participation by adolescent boys. A recreation involving bodies in ritualised combat is thus presented to members of youth as a site of male camaraderie, a source of identity, an arena of competition for prestige.

Swain (2001) asserts that football prowess represents the prestige resource in signifying 'successful' masculinity. The next chapter relates how competitive the boys were. They were keen to emphasise their sporting prowess in football and the sport had a significant role in collective constructions of identity. Talk of football was dominated by fighting and racism:

> Just racism really. It was really because one of the Asians, we were playing football and some white guy come up and took the football and he goes 'give it back'. He goes 'No'. and he goes 'give it back' and he goes 'No you Paki'. All of em just started then ... I was in a lesson ... called me out all of 'em did. I went out all of 'em like ... you start it first ... I just went up like ... I started first. It was this proper tall lad. I punched him in his face and he just fell on the floor ... and all of 'em jumped in and all the boys jumped and then after school they call their brothers and that down so we called all the Asians and that down so... (Sajid).

Drawing on Bourdieu's notions of capital and theory of distinction (1978, 1986), Shilling (2004:477) points to the impossibility of converting footballing prowess into economic, social or cultural capital. Footballing prowess also carries opportunity costs, and as with other working class dispositions, tends to have a negative impact on formal assessment as classic studies of education such as Bourdieu and Passeron, (1977) have shown. The prolonged investment in sport, especially football and associated fighting, earned the boys profits in the specific field of peer relations but negatively affected their educational outcomes. At Leyton, where academic expectations were low and job prospects few, football was a significant way of gaining and maintaining status among the peer group.

It is difficult to ascertain whether racialised tensions marked football out as the main event – as a contact sport, it allowed boys to vent their frustrations, which were blocked in the classroom, through the odd bad tackle, and this would inevitably escalate into a full fight. Whether racism was drawn on, as Yacoub suggests, as the last resort of beaten masculinities, is uncertain. Either way, football, fighting and racism were clearly entangled. Fights started with a glance, a glare or someone giving 'dirties' (dirty look) and this would often escalate into a huge free-for-all. Tensions ran extremely high after 9/11, when the boys felt particularly stigmatised.

'Snobs' are people who work

Researchers (see Martino, 1999; Renold, 2005) have also highlighted the normalising practices in which sexuality is deployed as a specific category for defining acceptable masculinity. Boys who demonstrate academic tendencies are often feminised, sexualised and demonised as 'poofters'. The boys did not employ sexist abusive language to Other academically successful students but gave them classed labels, such as 'snobs' – explained as 'people who work' (Arif). Abid managed to escape categorisation as Other. He was not part of the core group and avoided the major fights that positioned the boys involved as anti-education. Abid, however, was on the margins of the group and strategically took up a tough boy identity in the relative safety of some lessons. His strategic take up of hegemonic Asian masculinity enabled him to escape the label of 'snob' applied by some of the boys to those in the top sets, helped by his investment in cricket (see chapter 6), which had a special significance among the peer group.

School space

Researchers have noted how not only language but space and place in the school is used to signify exclusion and inclusion and related bullying practices (Nayak and Kehily, 1996; Epstein *et al*, 2001). School practices such as pupils' access to, and use of, physical spaces can be highly gendered (Skelton, 2000, 2001) and racialised, and the boys in this study talked about a racialisation of space both inside school and out. Boys report a 'policing of geographical territories' (Martino and Pallotta-Chiarolli, 2003:35) and boundaries in the school grounds and corridors. The boys in my study reported that in certain locations in the school they were no longer allowed to stand in groups of more than three because teachers perceived their collective bodies to be provocative and threatening – suggesting the enactment of the Asian gang. The boys complained bitterly that white boys had not been separated: 'They're still allowed to hang out in big groups but if there are more than three or four of us, they move us on' (Wahid).

In the playground, however, the boys claimed agency in carving out spaces they were able to own. The dominant Asian boys occupied the 'top end' near the fences while a group of footballing white boys took centre stage, occupying the bulk of the space in the main part of the playground. Groups of white girls and Asian girls and some mixed groups gathered nearby. It was not clear whether the Asian boys had been relegated to the outskirts of the playground but they justified their own location by the fences as due to the need to protect others. They could keep an eye on the 'little ones' and the Asian girls.

Arif:	Someone said something ... something to this guy who's in year 11 ... someone said something to his sister yeah and then it just kicked off ... he said something to that boy and that boy called him names then he called us lot
FS:	What happened?
Arif:	Nothing happened ... just Asian ... we sit cos like Asians hang on to the top and white people be at the bottom ... we run down and then all the teachers come ... too many teachers
FS:	So there are spaces...?
Arif:	... Asians see all the time what would happen
FS:	So they just keep separate. What happens if people cross?
Wahid:	Nothing really. They can cross but they [white students] never come up anyway

Conclusion

This chapter has revealed some of the complexities and struggles involved in maintaining status through 'tough boy' masculinities. The Asian boys' peer group was constructed externally, by a collective stigmatisation as trouble-makers, gang members or sometimes simply as Muslims. Internally, a range of cultural resources were drawn on to gain or refuse membership. In earlier research, Asian boys were constructed as Other and were feminised – either as academic achievers (Mac an Ghaill, 1994) or as 'weak' and/or 'effeminate' in teacher and pupil discourses (Connolly, 1998). Archer's research on Muslim Asian boys (2003) shows how they resisted the stereotypes and dominant discourses of weak Asian passivity by moving between black, Muslim and 'gangsta' masculinities to position themselves as strong and assertive within the school and in their local neighbourhood relations. The accounts discussed in this and the previous chapter also suggest a strategic repositioning between different identities in different contexts.

There appear to be two reasons for the dominance of Asian identities over Muslim identities in the context of peer relations. First, the external (school, peers, teachers, institutional, local media) construction of Asian boys as trouble-makers and violent gang members meant that Asian masculinity was constructed as powerful rather than weak, as it was in Archer's study. The boys' take up of Asian masculinity reinforced their newfound notoriety as strong and dangerous. So, in the local context, Asian masculinity was constructed as strong not weak.

Second, in the local context of peer relations within the Asian Muslim group, some boys were constructed as more authentically Muslim. These were the 'really religious' boys. Within the context of this local Muslim masculinity, a number of the activities, especially relationships with girls which gave the boys power and status within the school, were simultaneously constructed as illegitimate from a 'really religious' per-spective. Some of the boys talked about themselves as 'failed' Muslims (see chapter three).

Failed Muslim identities bolstered strong Asian identities – hetero-sexual attractiveness, smoking, going out – were all key markers of a strong masculine identity that was shared by the dominant white 'tough boys'. But it was racism and racialised differences that became an im-portant dividing line between the two groups of 'tough' school boys. The next chapter takes up themes of territory and turf, and the boys' heavy investments in their local identities.

5
Territory, turf and girls

Introduction

So far we have looked at the boys' strategic take up of a global community-focused Muslim identity that strives to counter the dominant discourses on the 'war on terror'. In the context of schooling, a 'tough' Asian male peer group identity was constructed in relation to the classed, gendered and racialised order of schooling. This chapter develops the theme on masculinities but in the context of locality and neighbourhood, where specific area-based masculinities cross-cut ethnic, religious and national ties and identities. As the boys' accounts reveal, these area-based identities were produced and contested in articulation with local histories, in the context of both local white working class neighbourhood struggles and Asian cultural and political struggles against far-right extremism and racism. A strong working class community ethos, emphasising loyalty and belonging, underscored the boys' struggles within and across local neighbourhoods. These area-based identities were strongly gendered. In this chapter, I discuss the demarcation of girls as symbolic markers of racialised boundaries in the masculine struggles over space and territory.

Territory and 'neighbourhood nationalisms'

As a number of analysts (Westwood, 1990; Cohen, 1993, 1996; Amin, 2002; Webster, 2003) note, working class urban masculinities are closely associated with locality as well as safety and danger. The boys in the study worked with strong ideas of which areas were 'safe' and 'dangerous', which were 'white', 'black' and 'Asian'. For example, the local cinema complex, referred to in the extract below, was identified as a dangerous space:

> Arif: Yeah outside school as well, like yesterday, we went to [local cinema complex]. These two older boys beeped at us and shouted 'Paki' and swore at us. We can't say nothing back – they're older than us ... So we just carried on walking. Then the next car that came up he did the same so ...
>
> FS: Two cars one after the other did the same?
>
> Arif: Yeah
>
> FS: How do you feel when that happens? What do you do?
>
> Wahid: We just ignore it. Because it happens all the time. It happens to all the boys.
>
> FS: What about girls?
>
> Wahid: No girls don't go there – it's too dangerous for them.

Arif and Wahid are talking about an area located on the boundary between Belstone and Newtown. The incident took place on a dual carriageway that led towards the main shopping centre on one side and the local cinema complex on the other. Wahid's construction of the area as simply 'too dangerous' for girls could be read as a defensive response or strategy to legitimise his own fear and his inability to strike back in the moment. However, as Webster (2003) and others have noted, it is most commonly at the borders of neighbourhoods such as Belstone and Newtown that fierce, often violent contestations take place over ownership, entry and belonging. It is because these areas have large, but by no means majority, ethnic minority populations that confrontations over space and territory ensue; producing 'neighbourhood nationalisms' (Hesse, 1992; Cohen, 1996; Werbner, 1996; Webster, 2003). Cohen refers to this as a racialisation of space which

> ... involves the colour coding of particular residential areas, housing estates or public amenities as 'white' or black in a way which often homogenises ethnically diverse neighbourhoods and turns relative population densities into absolute markers of racial division. This process is usually articulated through images of confrontation – 'front lines', 'no-go areas' and the like which serve to orchestrate moral panics about invasion; and 'blacks' taking over. (1996:71)

Researchers also argue that the presence of large numbers of British Asians in adjacent neighbourhoods has often been irrationally interpreted to fuel white fears that their neighbourhoods are being taken over and, by implication, that their whole way of life is under threat (Webster, 2004; Cohen, 1996; Amin, 2002). The incident Sajid and Hamid refer to below was sparked by the kinds of area-based fears Cohen refers to and had led to violent altercations between the police and Asian youth.

> Yeah there was a riot down Newtown and some people say now that there were some NFs [National Front] were gonna come down and like the news got around so like about 2 o'clock everyone gathered on Springfield road, the biggest road in Newtown yeah ... And then the police come down now yeah ... There's like quite a few ... of these guys coming down ... like these white people, NFs. Well, that's what everyone was saying ... The NF's here. They tried to get past the police but the police stopped 'em then like all these policeman start pushing these Asians so they start like fighting back throwing bottles at 'em and that and that's it. (Hamid)

Sajid describes another attempted 'march through' by far-right activists that had recently taken place on the border of Newtown:

Sajid: When the racist people come down ... I was there. Hundreds of police were there and they blocked the roads and they're standing by the shops and the buses going past and people threw bricks [laughs]

FS: Did you throw any?

Sajid: Yeah I did

FS: At the bus?

Sajid: At the coaches ... at the fascists. They were all just swearing

FS: Was there any fighting?

Sajid: No, they just went past.

Their willingness to come out fighting intersects with a history of organised local and national struggles against far-right incursions that relied nationally and locally on alliance building between ethnic minorities and the white left (Ramamurthy, 2006; Shain, 2009).

Boys cited such racist incursions as reasons for retreating to the safety of their own neighbourhoods and for their movement in large groups –

otherwise 'you might get jumped' (Aziz). However, as argued in the previous chapter, this movement in large groups was often irrationally interpreted as a threat due to notions of the 'Asian gang' (Alexander, 2000). This is not to say that the boys did not at times revel in their new-found notoriety as strong, tough boys who were not to be messed with. We have seen that they frequently glorified violence through their collective fight talk. However, both Belstone and Newtown were widely recognised as 'racial hotspots', and Newtown in particular was characterised by 'territorial stigmatisation' (Wacquant, 2008) where the presence of minority ethnic communities was both a cause and a symptom of its stigmatised 'ghettoised' status. The boys reported not only drugs, crime and prostitution but also racialised violence. Yacoub, a youth worker at Newtown, describes here the stigmatisation associated with belonging to the neighbourhood:

> When [people] come to Newtown, it's as if they've they come with fears ... Stereotypes. You've only got to look at the local newspaper ... three reports of a lad arrested from Newtown last week. They don't want to you to forget that this guy has been put away from Newtown, and he's Asian and it's just to feed these stereotypes ... word gets around and basically it's just how stereotypes are enforced onto other communities that have got nothing to do with Newtown. They don't even drive through. They don't even walk through it even. Newtown isn't on their path but they know *lots* about Newtown. They have no idea about Newtown, but they've certainly heard lots ... you know the young people; this is one of the things the lads are saying is that we're stigmatised. There's a negative stereotype about our people and about Newtown and about working class communities. It's so amazing to me that people as young as 13 and 14 are so clued up about these issues. But then it doesn't surprise me because that's their reality.

Yacoub's comments point to the role of the local media in perpetuating stereotypes about Newtown youth. He also suggests here that Newtown's reputation is possibly exaggerated by such media and outsider constructions of it. However, the reputation of the area was an important reference point for the boys in their constructions of local identities and their membership of the Newtown youth group:

> Because it keeps us off the street doesn't it? It keeps you off the street and hanging round with the wrong crowd ... and doing the wrong things ... because everyone knows that like they've got a lot of drugs ... Like there's a lot of drugs and prostitution ... besides it's too racist. (Arshad)

Racism was another factor, as Arshad's comment reveals. Youth provision was segregated in Newtown. The club was available to all youth in the area but was primarily used by Muslim Asian boys. Girls and white boys did not attend. Although in theory they could attend any of the local neighbouring clubs, in reality this was not a possibility. The boys reported that their attempts to interact with local white youth in neighbouring clubs were met with hostility, suspicion and racism. Racist name-calling was cited by some of the boys as a mechanism of excluding them. 'They called us curry monster ... and they called him a chocolate bum and him a chocolate soldier' said one. Another reported physical violence:

> Yeah I went to [another club in Oldwych] but then like a lot of fighting happened because we were Asians and they were whites and there were a lot of conflicts and because they ... the white workers couldn't interact with the Asians they had to call Aziz (Youth worker) which is wrong. Why call another Asian, because they're youth workers? They should be trained to deal with all different people. Why did they have call Aziz who lives in Newtown who knows these children – do you get me? There's no point. Why not just let the people who are working there deal with the Asian children? (Mudasser)

Mudasser's comments suggest they were treated by professional frameworks as a race apart. The retreat to the 'safety' of Newtown did result in segregation – but not the self-segregation implied in New Labour's policy discourses (Cantle, 2001). Rather, as the following comment reflects, several attempts were made to get youth to mix with each other but inevitably they ended in violent skirmishes. According to the boys, this was because racism had not been adequately dealt with. They claimed to have been willing to try out several of the initiatives that had been introduced, including playing football, but said this had inevitably ended in violent skirmishes. As the following account illustrates, masculine rivalries often resulted in racism being used in youthful masculine bids for power.

> You see, if that MP [David Blunkett] wants to get rid of all this racism and all that, how can that happen when incidents like Ashfields, when like all racism in schools and everything happen? First you've got to clean that up before you can get to communities ... that's true isn't it? You have to start at the bottom, and then work your way up. (Nadim)

The incident to which Nadim refers was a more formal 'cohesion' effort to bring local white and Asian youth to interact through a football match. But, as with many such attempts, an outbreak of violence brought a swift end to the day. Yacoub, the boys' youth worker, explained that 'some white kid went in with a really bad tackle that the referee ignored ... fighting broke out'. Speaking about another attempt to bring Asian and white youth together through football, he describes how such incidents normally arise and how he and his colleagues try to deal with them:

> When we were in the 'kick racism out of football' and we went to this other team. The white team said 'we've got this mate ... we've got this friend who's a gypsy ... so I hope you don't mind, but we call him Paki ... cos he's a tinker and he's dark. So if you don't mind, he's going to be playing and that's his name.' So, one of the Asian boys shouted out 'well one of my friends is Asian, but we call him Honkey Man, do you mind that? and they were like 'whoa!' And the Asian lads said 'we're just saying...' so as much as, whereas the Asian boys were the hot-heads and angry, we're trying to teach them ways of turning that aggression into positive. (Yacoub)

Yacoub's account suggests an interplay between biological and cultural notions of racism in the fierce contestations over space. 'Tinker' and 'Honkey' are racially charged biological terms of abuse that are drawn on by white and Asian boys to mark out territory. As Amin (2002) argues, it is often at the local level that differences are worked out and this seems to represent such an attempt to carve out differences from sameness. Les Back, too, notes 'common codes' between young white men and Asian men involved in the disturbances in the northern towns:

> A strong masculine culture that is hatred between young white men and young Asian men, mobilised by the riots. Their violent confrontations display a common aggressiveness, common 'gang' codes and a similar body language. Of course, this sameness is used to mark division, but only some aspects of this division are about ethnic cultural difference, with the rest about the frustrations of youth alienation and diminished social respects on both sides of the ethnic divide, the particularities of gang formation, the masculine protections of turf and territory. The trope of cultural segregation along ethnic lines take us only so far. (Cited in Amin, 2002:8)

As Back observes, and contrary to dominant policy discourses of segregation and community cohesion, cultural differences are not the cause of tensions and violent confrontations between working class young people, but they become markers of those tensions in young people's struggles to gain status and respect. It is in the context of changing times, when old certainties such as the transition from school to manual labour have all but disappeared and young men can no longer expect simply to step up into a breadwinner role (McDowell, 2002), that these 'masculine protections of turf and territory' come to hold such significance. They are simultaneously struggles for patriarchal status.

As discussed in the previous chapter, football prowess empowers boys who have nothing else by which to define themselves as successful. This was just as true in local matches as it was in the kick around about school. As Yacoub explains:

> That's the only positive thing they have in their lives, that is. So they put everything into it. They haven't lost a game so every white side wants to beat Newtown ... nobody can beat them. They haven't got the discipline that these boys have. They haven't got what these boys have come from. It's not in their reality. They don't have to fight as hard. So when they go and play them ... honest to God it's like seeing ... our lads are like 14-16. It's like seeing five 22-year-old David Beckhams play six-year-olds ... it's not a game ... They're there to win. It's a pattern we see nation-wide. (Yacoub)

> ***

> Riaz: We won the power league in the football and ...

> Yasser: ...Yeah we had a fight with against these *goray*, yeah

> ***

> Arshad: You know because my mate scored a good goal he goes to him 'you Paki , you black bastard' and then there was a big fight innit, eh ?

> Mudasser: We got battered but we battered the *goray*. It was funny, Little Saleem was going for really going for it .... extreme racism

We can see that football, fighting and racism were inseparable. Local matches, like the school matches, were often abandoned before the final whistle had blown because of fighting.

Girls

Local space was not just racialised or colour-coded but also gendered, so the places the boys hung out were constructed as either unsafe or out of bounds for girls. The exclusion of girls and women from public space was partly a re-worked carry-over from older localised uses of public space. For example, community struggles, including antiracist activism, have often gone hand in hand with, if not necessitated, a macho stance that simultaneously objectifies and marginalises women. In the aftermath of the Rushdie affair, for example, members of the feminist group, Women Against Fundamentalism, claimed to face the macho and misogynistic stance of the anti-Rushdie protestors (WAF, 1989; Siddiqui, 1991). Harwant Bains (1988), writing about the Southall Youth Movement (SYM), comments on how the group's formation to both Fascists and the perceived passivity of an elder generation produced the SYM's particular style of machismo:

> This reproduces the patriarchal attitudes towards women to be found amongst elders throughout the community. Any girl who tries to take an active part in the running of SYM is popularly regarded as 'loose' with the consequences that those who do try to get involved very quickly leave. When the leadership is challenged about its attitudes to women they simply reply that they were brought up that way and are too old to change. At the same time their street culture supports the symbolic transformation of the Sikh warrior into the modern 'street fighting man' a 'macho' pose directed as much against the passivity of the older generation as against racist skinheads and the NF. (Bains, 1988:237)

For the Newtown group, footballing rivalries and individualised and collective struggles against racism often went hand in hand with displays of hyper-heterosexual masculinity. For example, the boys reported that an Asian girl who had recently attempted to join the club had not returned after her first visit:

FS: So, this is an all boys group, right?

Arshad: A girl did come once but she didn't come after that

Mushtaq: Could have screwed her here

Arshad: ... Oi don't man

Mushtaq: What? I could have had her right over there

Arshad's attempts to censor Mushtaq's hyper-heterosexual performance reveal his acute awareness of the inappropriate nature of his display. The attempt to censor was perhaps due more to my presence in the group as a woman and older Muslim 'sister'. While there were some other explicit sexual references such as 'White girls are down for a bag of brown stuff' (Riaz), the boys mostly avoided making such explicitly sexual references in my company.

Archer (2003) talks about the role of the researcher in the production and contestation of identities in the interview context. When she herself interviewed boys they were less forthcoming on issues of racism than they were with the Asian woman who assisted Archer with her research. The boys asserted strong patriarchal identities in relation to this Asian female researcher.

Likewise it could be argued that boys were more willing to talk about politics and racism because of my perceived status as a fellow Muslim. However, I found the boys more willing to talk about gender in the earlier group discussions when a male researcher (BG) was present than when I interviewed them alone. My status as an older 'sister' had an inhibiting effect.

These boys did not construct girls as 'mental' and out of control, as they did in Archer's (2003) study. Neither did they talk directly about women being the 'height of respect' as in Hopkins' (2005) study. They did, however, at times display the 'sexist equality' that Hopkins talks about, as in Zahid's account of why girls should be allowed to continue into education (see chapter seven). Others also mentioned that girls could go to university, as many of their sisters had, as long as they did not become 'corrupt' – which generally meant as long they did not engage in 'western' style relationships with boys.

White girls were mostly referenced in relation to struggles and competition with white boys:

> See the thing was ... When we went there, they [white boys] weren't better than us in table tennis, they weren't better than us in pool and when we played football against them they thought they were better than us but then we proved 'em wrong. And we beat 'em at that, that just topped it off, that just put the cherry on the cake. (Arshad)
>
> ***
>
> Nadim: we would talk to the girls but the boys wouldn't talk to us and they didn't like it that we were talking to their girls and Tariq was doing something naughty with one of 'em so...

FS: So, what happened?

Nadim: It all kicked off didn't it?

Ramji (2007) argues that Muslim young men in her study saw white girls as 'easy' and relationships with them were pursued as a way of 'getting one over' on white boys. Dating a Sikh or Hindu girl was seen as the ultimate way of 'getting one over on an old adversary'. There were few Sikh and Hindu and girls in Newtown but interactions with white girls were commonly cited as symbols of masculinity in competitive racialised fight talk. In group interviews boys were more likely to construct girls in highly sexualised terms, again as part of group bonding. But in individual interviews, boys often talked in less objectivised ways about white girls as part of their friendship groups, as long term girlfriends and even as potential partners in their imagined futures (see chapter seven). If Yacoub's account is to be believed, it seems that in local inter-masculine rivalries Asian boys had become the 'new black' (Alexander, 2000).

> The young kids are treated as foreigners so they're seen as different. So they're seen as something else. The young girls then, are looking for their kicks and so they're heading for the Asian lads and white lads don't like stuff like that because they've again become European and territorial about *their* girls and suddenly they care about them. So it causes a whole range of everyday realities for the Asian lads. (Yacoub)

Yacoub observes that one of the consequences of being stigmatised as 'bad boys' is that the new-found sense of danger is highly attractive to white girls. White girls, then, collude in the production of this hegemonic form of racialised masculinity (Connell, 2005). Yacoub's account positions white girls as agentic, if predatory (they head for the boys), but at the same time denies agency to the boys who are targeted and have no choice but to consent. At the same time it positions girls as symbols of masculinity or as markers of racialised boundaries (Anthias and Yuval Davis, 1992) in masculine struggles over territory and turf.

Yacoub's account also invokes colonial fears about interracial mixing, because there is a need to preserve ethnic purity (Ware, 1992). These fears were re-worked in the context of the Notting Hill and Nottingham riots, in the 1960s, when newspaper reports blamed the sight of a white women walking with a black man as the cause of the violence. As we saw earlier, these fears have resurfaced through media and political representations of rape crimes involving Asian men, for example, through Thilo Sarrazin's tenuous connections between the restrictions of Islamic culture and the apparent tendency for Turkish Muslim youth in Germany to target white women (Kreikenbaum, 2010), and Jack Straw's and Ann Cryer's similar comments in relation to Pakistani heritage boys in England.

At the same time as white girls were constructed as 'available', Asian girls were relationally constructed as 'out of bounds':

FS:	But you don't mind ... other people talking about girls
Sajid:	No not really. My mate Hussein, there he might go out with a girl [laughs]
FS:	Would you?
Sajid:	I've been out with a few girls
FS:	Are they English or Pakistani?
Sajid:	English, and I won't go with Pakistanis because end of the day you know the brothers ...[laughs] you get beat up. It's not worth it [laughs]

Asian girls were mostly referenced through a discourse of protection. For example, certain areas were considered 'too dangerous' for them to be in – though it could be that such discourse also helped to legitimate the boys' exclusion of girls from public space and the discursive construction of the home as a safe (feminine) space, that is, to defend patriarchal privilege.

Aziz:	Over stupid things like I don't know why ... if we're just standing there and just glance at somebody they, you know how boys are ... Over a stupid thing like that a minor thing like that or when someone swears at somebody or they swear at Asian girls or cussing them
FS:	So you stick up for other people?
Aziz:	I stick up for anybody ... white, Asian, I got a lot of white friends ... I stick up for them. My friends are white boys and Asian boys but if someone cusses my sisters' friends or Asian girls then I get a bit offended, they're like my sisters. I get offended ... a minor thing like that

In constructing white girls as acceptable girlfriends, they simultaneously constructed Asian girls as out of bounds and thus themselves as protectors of Asian femininity. Through appropriating the discourse of protection, however, the boys denied agency to Asian girls. These constructions are interesting when compared with the views of Asian and Muslim girls (Shain, 2003). This research found that Asian girls often castigated Asian boys for their relationships with white girls, suggesting it was part of their incorporation into dominant white culture. Asian girls were not passive but also extremely willing and able to fight their own battles (*ibid*).

Newtown versus Belstone: it's a territorial thing

Not only were masculine rivalries racialised but the boys' strong investments in local identities as Newtowners or Belstoners or Rytoners often led to other forms of neighbourhood nationalism. For example, some boys reported that once at college rivalries became less centred on race and more area-based, which often meant Asian boys fought with each other:

Aziz:	Like the first years had a football match with second years and they fouled one of the players ... and they just had a fight
FS:	When they play football are they from the same area?
Aziz:	No they're from different areas ... that's what causes the trouble ... Ashfields, Ryton. Mainly Ashfields cause the trouble and Newtown and Belstone
FS:	Is it that important where they come from?
Aziz:	I'm not really bothered but for some people it matters ... Ashfielders, Belstoners

***

Asad:	Well it's just the stupid stuff like football. Like they'll say 'you fouled me' and he'll say 'no I didn't' and they'll say 'I'll break their legs', they say 'come on' and they'll have 50 people behind one guy and 50 people behind the other and then one thing leads to another – some people will die
FS:	Is that Whites and Asians?
Asad:	No! Asian on Asian!
FS:	Why do you think that happens?

108

Asad: I don't know [laughs] it's weird isn't it? I think they're trying to show who's harder. It's all this big headedness

Assad points to masculine rivalries centring on the need to prove who is toughest. A possible factor in the de-racialisation of college fights here was also the numerical significance of a more diversified group of Asian boys. The college drew in boys from a wider catchment area than the school and as so the familiarity and intimacy that boys experienced in the context of schooling was not readily available at college. Relationships with Asian girls were also (covertly) accepted and sometimes the reasons for fights. But the main source of fighting seemed, ostensibly at least, to centre on contestations over territory and turf.

Mudasser: He comes from Newtown but he moved out to Ryton but he's a bit of an outcast ...

Nasim: And he was born in Afghanistan, weren't you?

Nadim: I know that there's not many people who like each other from other estates but because I was born in Ashfields, and most of the Ashfields people know that I was born in Ashfields so they'll still treat me with the same respect as they treat other Ashfieders. Newtown still treat me as a Newtowner so I know where I am in them two places

FS: What about Belstone?

Nadim: Well my dad has got a lot of friends and I know a lot of Belstone people through my dad and I know a lot of people in Belstone through my dad cos he knows their dads through my dad. So if they have gang wars then I don't get involved

Mudasser and Nasim are conflating local and national ethnic identities, making no distinction between being from Newtown or Ryton or from Afghanistan. In many other accounts too, the local differences were greater than national ones. The boys were fiercely local at times, for example several replied to the question of where they were born by naming the hospital they were born in. This symbolic ownership of the local area was significant in their claims to belonging in the local area. These area-based allegiances are a historical carry-over from pre-immigration times and in this sense could be read as specifically Oldwych concerns.

As Avtar Brah has argued,

The lived cultures that young Muslim[s] inhabit are highly differentiated according to such factors as country of origin, rural/urban background prior to migration, regional and linguistic background in the subcontinent, class position in the subcontinent as well as in Britain, and regional location in Britain. British Asian cultures are not simply a carry over from the (country of origin) ... Hence Asian cultures of London may be distinguished from their counterparts in Birmingham. Similarly, east London cultures have distinctive features as compared with those from west London. (Brah, 1993:448-9)

'Niggers' v 'Teps'

Dress, language and style were important markers of localised area identities. Newtown boys, for example, appropriated black cultural forms and styles and were, as the following account suggests, labelled as 'niggers'. Newtown, unlike Belstone, has a significant African-Caribbean population and the boys' appropriation of black cultural styles reflected their incorporation into the dominant culture of the area. A Newtown style was appropriated by black, Asian and white youth as a marker of belonging to the area. Belstone historically had a more transient population, most notably because of the location of a university and student residences in what was known as the Asian part of the neighbourhood. It also had a larger population of asylum seekers and refugees. The boys displayed strong associations with the local, town and ward areas in which they lived. Local masculinities are produced in articulation with local histories and geographies, as Yacoub's words illustrate:

The only common factor was that we're Muslim ... But the differences [in perception between the youth of both neighbourhoods] were ... Right, from Belstone ... The thing about Newtown is that they all dress like niggers'. Newtown, 'The thing about Belstone is that they're all well-behind ... proper typical Pakis' so this is what these are labelling theories that come from the European side ... We call it area-ism.

'Typical Pakistani' (sometimes shorted to 'Tep' or TP) is an internally contested, mildly derogatory term applied by Pakistanis to other Pakistanis. It generally signifies stereotypical characteristics associated with Pakistani identities. TP is area-based and varies through time. For example, in Qureshi's (2004) study with Edinburgh Pakistanis in the late 1990s, TP was contested as elsewhere but cohered around gendered notions of stereotypical Pakistani behaviour. For girls the key signifiers were: bleached/streaked hair, coloured contact lenses, bright red lipstick and overdressing for university. For boys, typical markers included an obsession with mobile phones, pagers and hair gel. In the current study, TP or 'Tep' was appropriated by Bengali boys too. For example, Asad said he did not want his future wife to be 'typical'. Specific markers of 'Tepness' included consumption of Bollywood, boys wearing loud shirts tucked into tight jeans and a lack of street fashion and culture. Most commonly, Tepness was applied as a derogatory term to signify and subordinate others who lacked fashion sense or were not streetwise. 'Tep' was not an identity that was accepted readily – and if there were boys who liked Bollywood, they did not admit it.

Farood (quite newly arrived from Afghanistan) initially admitted to watching Hindi films but promptly retracted this, possibly because of the negative characterisations of Bollywood style among the Asian boys' peer group but perhaps also because it did not sit easily with notions of academic success. As he says – 'if I'm watching Hindi films then why am I not studying?'

Another possible reason was that Bollywood consumption was feminised by the boys and largely associated with mums, sisters and the home. 'My sisters are always watching these Indian films' (Asad); 'they play this loud Hindi music, it's dead annoying' (Abid).

Bollywood is consumed by Asian Muslims as well as Hindus and Sikhs, but among Muslims Bollywood remains contested, with groups such as *Hizbu'Tahrir* (HT) asserting that it is largely an Indian Hindu and Sikh project for assimilating Muslims. Early HT literature was scathing of Bollywood. In one of their leaflets in the 1990s, 'Asian born to be brown', they challenged the notion of a collective Asian identity, claiming that this collective identity was modelled on Indian, not Muslim, cultural tastes and habits. Such collective cultures, said the leaflets, were based on the eradication of Islam and that activities such as 'going out night clubbing' represented an Indian pursuit of acceptance into British society on the terms of the host society.

Conclusion

This chapter has focused on the boys' accounts of their neighbourhood experiences. The data presented shows their strong investment in local area identities that are sometimes racialised and sometimes not. I have suggested that area-based struggles have a history in Oldwych. For example, white working class struggles over territory and space are a carry-over from pre-immigration white 'ownership' of the local area. There is also a history of black antiracist struggles which, in the 1970s and 1980s, centred around the workplace and unions, now expressed in street based fights and protests since those resources have disappeared. Kundnani (2001:107) writes that by the 1990s the new generation of young Asians were unwilling to accept racism meted out to older generations:

> When racists came to their streets for a fight, they would meet violence with violence. And with the continuing failure of the police to tackle racist gangs, violent confrontations between groups of Whites and Asians became more common. Inevitably, when the police did arrive to break up a meleé, it was the young Asians who bore the brunt of police heavy-handedness. As such, Asian areas became increasingly targeted by the police as they decided that gangs of Asian youths were getting out of hand.

Contrary to individualisation thesis which suggests declining ties at local level in terms of tradition and community, the boys were forming collective identities that centred on both Asian and local working class notions of community. Working out differences at a local level was part of the building of collective identities. It is through these neighbourhood nationalisms that the boys formed strong connections with and ownership of the local area in ways that sometimes cross-cut racial and ethnic identities. Their struggles over ownership and belonging in the local area, whether expressed through football struggles or fighting, help otherwise disadvantaged and marginalised young men to demonstrate status among their contemporaries (Earle and Philips, 2009).

6

Leisure, sport and music

Introduction

This chapter explores themes of race, nation and culture as articulated in the boys' discussions about their leisure and their cultural preferences and affiliations. The chapter has three sections. The first considers the boys' leisure activities and in particular their gendered and racialised constructions of leisure, the second their sporting affiliations and the significance of sport in their constructions of difference at local level. The third part discusses the topic of music and style and the boys' appropriation or rejection of particular styles. Educational identities are located in broader cultural and popular discourses of masculinity, race, class, identity and style.

Leisure

When asked about their out of school activities, typical home activities included 'watching TV with my dad' (Nadim), reading the Quran (Zahid), 'playing on the computer' (Younis). Farood presented as one of the most studious boys and, in the privacy of the individual interview, was keen to talk about how much studying he was doing. In group contexts talk of politics, racism, and football dominated the discussion. 'When I'm not at school I just go to the library ... then go home and do my homework and after that I watch television and then sleep'. However he also confessed to 'watching *EastEnders* and Hindi films'.

Two of the 'really religious' boys, Zahid and Umar, talked about the importance of reading the Quran and praying at home as part of their daily

113

out of school activities. 'Visiting cousins and having them over to us' (Umar) was another home activity. However, most leisure activities took place outside of the home. Home was constructed as a feminine space and interaction with sisters and mothers was rarely mentioned in the context of leisure. Samad (1998) accounts for boys' use of outside space as due to widespread overcrowding in Asian homes with large families. He maintains that boys are sent out because there is insufficient space for them in the home. An important gendered dimension to the use of space is missed in this classed and racialised explanation of boys' leisure. Only one of the boys mentioned domestic chores in discussion about 'home' activities: 'I play snooker or go out to the cinema or do things like for my mum like go and get shopping from Morrisons or like wash the dishes ... and other chores at home' (Wasim).

Wasim, whose father worked in a restaurant, was one of the boys who formed the inner core of the Asian boys' peer group and although he said this in an individual interview, it does suggest the contradictory subject positions taken up by the boys. For example, in peer relations, being tough and macho was all-important, yet, in the private interview, Wasim talked comfortably about an activity that might have provoked ridicule from his friendship group.

Most of the boys' leisure activities were conducted outside the home away from family and, importantly, their sisters. Football and cricket were most commonly cited as out of school leisure activities. For some, this involved playing in the local park and in a Power League five-a-side tournament. This brought them into contact with 'Italians, blacks and white people' in neighbouring areas, often involving the tense fighting described in previous chapters as part of the struggle to assert their masculinities. Others played in the local park, 'just having a kick around' (Mudasser). Other pastimes included going to the mosque – not always to pray but sometimes to meet friends – and leisure pursuits such as 'go[ing] shopping or walk around with my mates' (Ibrahim), playing pool and table tennis, 'hanging about either down the park or up Oldwych' (Habib), 'messing about having a laugh' (Nadim).

These reflected typical working class leisure pursuits revolving around 'hanging around about doing nothing' and they have been romanti- cised in the past by youth researchers (Hall and Jefferson, 1976; Corrigan, 1979; Willis, 1977) as providing economically deprived boys with cultural knowledge of the way to become a working class man (Mac-Donald and Marsh, 2005). According to Corrigan (1976), 'doing nothing' constituted probably the largest and most complex youth subculture of all and provided space for counter-hegemonic identities to develop. Through recent policy discourses focusing on 'respect', however, 'hanging about doing nothing' has been reclassified in highly unromantic terms as anti-social behaviour and the subject of heavy policing and criminalisation.

For the boys in this study, much 'hanging about' was centred on the entrance to the local shopping centre, especially on Saturdays – but they also hung around the local cinema complex, places away from their residential areas where they could impress local (usually white) girls. Willis (1990) suggests that 'doing nothing' requires effort and symbolic creativity, especially in 'looking good'. For the boys in my study, it required money for the right kind of clothing and the right designer labels. As Tariq said, 'just like image, you really need to show off a bit'. Sajid explained why he spends a great deal of effort and money from his restaurant job on 'dressing the part':

Sajid: When I'm not with my mates playing football I just wear ... sportswear like tracksuit bottoms and top and trainers. But when I'm going out with me mates it's design wear *Versace* and all that [laughs]

FS: Are labels important? Why?

Sajid: To me like, because if you're walking down around town and you've got some you know ... cheap clothes on and everyone's like thinking what a gyppo or something. So I always buy my own clothes. Really, my mum's not paying for it; I'm paying for it myself because I get £120 so I just pay myself ...

Sajid draws on a racist term of abuse, 'gyppo', commonly used in the local area to signify asylum seekers. In Oldwych there had recently been a rise in the refugee and asylum seeking community and this had been the focal concern of far-right extremism. Sajid was keen to distinguish his style from what he called the 'charity shop' style of these newly arrived groups. In parallel with the distinctions made between 'niggers' and 'teps' (see chapter 5), there was an ongoing production of difference at local level (Amin, 2002) and one example of racialised dissociation. Surprisingly little racism was expressed towards asylum seekers and Traveller communities in the interviews. But during my fieldwork visits in Belstone I was witness to obvious racialised hostility from locals, including one shopkeeper, towards newly arrived communities. In media discussions and debates too, there has been an increasing tendency among Asian communities to position themselves as indigenous Britons, calling for a halt to immigration.

Sajid invested heavily in his physical appearance, ploughing a significant amount of the money he earned in his restaurant job into 'looking good'. As well as routinely hanging around with mates, Eid day presented another arena for male bonding:

Saleem: I go out with my mates really and have a good time that's it really

FS: Where do you go?

Saleem: We go anywhere. Like last Eid, we hired a car like and went to London and then up to Manchester. When we got back we just basically went down the park

Eid became a racialised masculine arena, 'a chance to spend time with male friends, travel outside the area away form the gaze of the family and community, to drive fast cars, talk to girls, stay out all night', as Alexander noted (2000:133).

Sporting affiliations

Sport is recognised as an important signifier of nation and nationalism. In the 1990s, Conservative minster Norman Tebbit sparked a row about identity when he suggested that ethnic minority allegiance to their 'home' cricket team signalled a rejection of Britishness. Tebbit said that, 'If you come to live in a country and take up the passport of that country and you see your future and your family's future in that country, it seems to me that is your country, you just can't keep harking back' (cited in Werbner, 1996:104).

The significance of sport in the construction and contestation of identities has been noted by a number of researchers (Hoberman, 1986; Jarvie, 1990; MacClancy, 1996). As MacClancy (1996:2) observes, sports are 'vehicles of identity, providing people with a sense of difference and a way of classifying themselves and others, whether latitudinally or hierarchically'. Hoberman (1986) notes a tendency among sports fans to construct their sporting heroes as 'proxy warriors'. Nayak (2003) and McDowell (2002) have posited the significance of football, both in terms of affiliations and the bookish knowledge required to master it, as a major means of building working class solidarity in new times, that is, in the context of deindustrialised labour markets and the feminisation of service industries which have supposedly left men out in the cold. The counter-hegemonic role of football club affiliation in providing working class solidarity (Jones, 1988) is stressed, but football has long had connotations of hooliganism and nationalism (Hargreaves, 1990), as discussed below.

Being able to talk about football was significant for the construction of schoolboys' masculinities. Arif identified football as a tool for engaging in discussions with the white boys in his group in one of the higher sets: 'I follow like football because like ... you can have a conversation with the white boys ... all the white people talk about it so we can have a conversation' (Arif).

In Leyton school, football talk, as opposed to practice, was largely a preserve of the white boys. In the interviews, playing football was more significant than being able to talk about it. Most did not support local teams, as the white boys in school did. Only a minority supported local English teams and despite their strong Newtown and Belstone identities (see chapter five), only one, Yasser – who described himself as mixed race: white English and Pakistani – talked about supporting a local Oldwych team. There was a marked difference between Asian boys and English white boys in this respect. White boys engaged in fierce battles over which of the two Oldwych teams warranted support. Unlike white boys, none of the Muslim or Asian boys watched live matches. Yasser had been, but stopped going because it was 'too racist'.

Yasser:	I used to go
Arshad:	But they called you Paki didn't they?
FS:	What was like? ...
BG:	But you don't like to go?
Yasser:	They're racist

None of the other boys supported a local Oldwych team. One supported Manchester United 'because they've got the glamour' (Asad) and another, Arsenal 'because my cousins are from London' (Sajid). No other English team received the support of the Muslim boys. Real Madrid was cited by Asad as a team worthy of support because of its Brazilian players. None of the boys confessed to actively supporting the national England team. This finding differs from that of Bagguley and Hussain (2007), who found that at the time of the 2002 World Cup, St. George flags became a common sight in Bradford. They report that taxi drivers and local residents were displaying active Englishness. This was not the case for the boys in my study, almost all of whom expressed support for Brazil as a national team and for 'anyone other than England'.

Burdsey (2007) too notes an increase in support for England among Asians in the last decade and suggests this is in part due to the breakthrough of some Asian, mainly mixed race English and Indian, players. Asian Indians, especially Hindus who are the most socioeconomically advantaged of British Asian communities, may well be accepting Englishness as part of their identity but this was not true of the Muslim boys in the study. Indians have also been constructed, through anti-Muslim racism, as the more acceptable face of Asian Britain, and extremist groups such as the English Defence League have used Indians to front their cause. For Pakistanis, Bangladeshis and other Muslims who are located in some of the poorest and most racially tense neighbourhoods, such feelings of belonging are challenged on a daily basis through, for example, the violent displays of Englishness expressed on football terraces (Back *et al*, 1998; Carrigan *et al*, 1998). The need to avoid such violent confrontations in yet another sphere could explain the lack of support for local teams.

The most commonly cited reason for not supporting England was 'cos English are rubbish' but the lack of Muslim Asian players could also be a factor. The boys cited the skill and flair of Brazilian players to justify their support of the Brazilian team. Sajid, who supported Arsenal, also expressed strong support for the Brazilian team:

Sajid: Brazil ... they're an excellent team they have really good players. They're just always winning like. Because you know they might win so you gotta support em. I've got a few tops at home. Three of em and I've got about five Arsenal shirts

FS: Yeah? Who's your favourite Arsenal player?

Sajid: Thierry Henry

FS: Why him?

Sajid: He's very good Miss. He's always getting into the game and passing to other people so they have a chance to score like. And he scores a few himself like every game.. They played em some, I think it was Moscow, and they've drawn them but they did try hard

Collectively supporting Brazil, a successful, skilful team, enabled the boys to win status in discussions with white boys about football and to counter exclusionary discourses of Englishness. They were able to dismiss England, and by association white boys at school, as 'rubbish' by comparison with Brazil. Supporting teams that could not possibly be watched live, could also be read as a strategy to avoid exclusionary and often violent displays of Englishness. Back *et al* (1998) and Burdsey (2007) have researched the violent displays of Englishness associated with football support and report that chants such as 'die Paki' and 'we're coming to get you fucking Pakis' are common among English football supporters. During his research, Burdsey (2007) observed a group of English supporters charging aggressively at a car full of Asian supporters.

What most appeals to Sajid about a player such as Henry is his team (community/collective) spirit. He is constructed as the successful but still somehow the Other of competitive individualism which is embedded in education and which the boys associated negatively with white family structures and cultures. This construction of Henry as a team player resonated strongly with the community ethos invoked by the boys' friendships, and with notions of strong cohesive Asian families vis-a-vis weak, individualistic families.

The rejection of England and Englishness was not fixed, however. When asked who they would support if England were playing Turkey, less than one third chose Turkey over England. Interestingly, the notion of a global Muslim brotherhood did not stretch to supporting Turkey. Although they could not articulate why, it is quite possibly because of the construction of Turks as different and westernised. This did not lead to rejection of individual Turkish boys, as Ibrahim was included on the margins of the Asian boys' group. And possibly, in the aftermath of the flotilla incident in 2010 when nine Turks were killed by Israeli soldiers aboard a freedom flotilla in international waters on its way to Gaza, Turkey might be considered more supportable. However, another significant and contradictory finding was the preference in almost every case (Arif aside) for England over Germany.

FS: What about national teams? Do you support England?

Abid: [Emphatically shaking his head] Brazil

FS: Why Brazil?

Abid: Cos English are rubbish

FS: If England are playing Germany who would you support?

Abid: It would have to be England but I wouldn't support the team. Football isn't really important to me as a national game but cricket is like in the national game I like when Pakistan are playing, I really like watching em

FS: If England was playing Brazil?

Asad: Brazil

FS: If England was playing Turkey?

Asad: Turkey

FS: Germany?

Asad: Probably England

FS: What's the difference between Turkey and Germany?

Asad: I don't know. You just go on your instincts

According to Giulianotti and Armstrong (1997:11), 'football centres upon an affirmation of faith, an element of identity, both personal and collective, that is never fully communicable in effectively rational terms' and there are obviously complex factors in operation. One factor could relate to racialised associations with 'Nazi' Germany, which remain a hangover from the Second World War but are still featured in the English school history curriculum. Moreover, 'hatred' for Germany and German football is a strong marker of Englishness that is embedded in the school. As Amin (2002) notes, ethnic minority boys have been schooled in a British imperialist curriculum since the age of four so it is hardly surprising that they have internalised such core English values.

Muslim boys, then, performed English identities through their lack of support for the German football team. The one boy who chose Germany over England was Arif, because he wished to engage in competitive football talk with white boys: 'originally I'd say England but just to piss the white people off I'd say Germany' (Arif).

Cricket

As Abid's account indicates, cricket was considered the national game by most of the Pakistani and Bangladeshi boys in the study and they invariably supported Pakistan. Burdsey (2007) argues that supporting a South Asian nation has an important function for many British Asians. It facilitates the construction of an 'imagined community' (Anderson, 1991), in that it forges a symbolic link with the subcontinent. This fosters the celebration of tradition and feelings of belonging with the nation from which they or their forbearers migrated.

Second, through cricket fandom British Asians can distance themselves from those elements of 'Englishness' with which they feel uncomfortable. As Werbner points out (1996:101, cited in Burdsey, 2007), 'it is in the field of sport, through support of the national [Pakistani] team, that young British Pakistanis express their love of both cricket and the home country, along with their sense of alienation and disaffection from British society'.

Racial tensions on the school playing field are often felt off the field (Shain, 2003). A construction of Pakistanis as 'cheats' filters through into schooling but also polarises and prevents their supporting England. Support for Pakistan, India, Sri Lanka and Bangladesh may also be a rejection of the version of Englishness that is passed on through cricket.

Whereas Englishness in football is often constructed through notions of hooliganism, another form of Englishness is present in cricket that is equally exclusionary. Williams (2000:46) argues that 'Cricket has often been celebrated as a symbol of Englishness. The match on the village green is still depicted as the purest form of cricket and used to create an immediately recognisable image of England'. Williams maintains that 'cricket's supposed tradition of sportsmanship and fair play has been seen as congruent with Christian teachings but also as an expression of a distinctively English sense of moral worth'. These forms of Englishness are very much associated with a white England, 'with Englishness as a white moral capacity and, given the imperial dimension of international cricket, had an important role in providing a moral justification for Empire' (p48-9). A rejection of the English national cricket team could be read as a rejection of Empire. In the context of colonial subordination and contemporary racism, Carrington *et al* (1998) suggest that international cricket can operate for British Asians as a means of cultural resistance.

The connections with Empire and the divisions created between India and Pakistan by colonial regimes in India could perhaps explain the intense competition between India and Pakistan on and off the pitch. For example, in 1992, a floodlit match between India and Pakistan in London was abandoned because of fighting (Williams, 2000). Pakistan was the national side for virtually all the boys but, interestingly, support for the England team was more forthcoming than support for India.

> Pakistan of course [laughs] England's before India. Just a case of the history of Pakistan and India (Zahid, Leyton)
>
> ***
>
> FS: What if England was playing India?
>
> Abid: England definitely (emphatically)
>
> FS: Why's that?
>
> Abid: Yeah and I but ...... You're not Indian are you?
>
> FS: No
>
> Abid: I just *don't* like Indians. I just hate em. I just really don't like em at all. No. I like just ... the things they ... Indians are totally different from Pakistanis. Like some Indians get called Pakis not because they're being racist English people. Yeah I'm saying 'why are you calling them that? They're totally different from us. They do other stuff like'. It's definitely a different country, India is from Pakistan
>
> FS: What do they do that's different?
>
> Abid: They drink. I don't like that
>
> FS: Do you know any Indians
>
> Abid: I used to but I don't know them anymore well I know 'em but I don't really see them any more

122

It seems that for Abid, being called a Paki is more acceptable than being identified with Indians. Indians are not worthy of the label Paki because they are different. Abid temporarily subverts the racist term of abuse. As Abid's and Zahid's accounts suggest, sporting affiliations provided another context for the discursive production of sameness and difference. This ordering, sorting and sifting of sameness and difference helped to cement local bonds through the identification of hate figures and Others.

Playing cricket, like playing football, was a significant factor in the production, regulation and contestation of masculinities, as the following quotes demonstrate. By playing, they are able to produce strong, skilful identities and at the same time subordinate weaker, less skilled boys. Rafiq talks about how Habib is scared of the ball so they have to compensate and bowl slowly. Normally cricket is fast, hard, and so powerful that the ball could knock you out. Habib measures up in terms of fighting but does not possess enough sporting capital.

Rafiq: Yeah me an Wasim go to the school cricket team most of the time. Habib came once. He can't even play and it was really funny ... he was just scared of the ball. The opposite team bowl so fast it will break your legs

FS: Really?

Rafiq: We just bowl slow and everyone says what are you doing that for? Bowl him hard

FS: Is that Hamid?

Rafiq: Yeah ... Quite tough

Cricket is often constructed through its association with upper class masculinity and the slow pace of the game, so is more feminised than football. So it is interesting to note Rafiq's references to bowling fast and hard as a way of winning back masculinity through the game. Abid also said cricket was not played 'properly' in the school. The use of a soft orange ball (presumably to avoid injuries) was seen as a significant point of racial discrimination in school but also supported Abid's own assertion of hegemonic Asian masculinity within the context of the peer group:

Cricket team ... I was supposed to be playing on Tuesday, supposed to be playing with a corky, but we but we didn't, so I didn't play. They gave us this great big orange thing ...

This annoys me and our boys always come to the practices ... 20 people came ... They were all English people ... and they got on to the team and even though they don't come to practice they picked them

---

This school's a bit rubbish, you know the private schools have a proper tournament.

Music

Archer and Yamashita (2003) found, in their study of inner city masculinities, that boys from varied ethnic backgrounds took up black cultural forms and styles to perform what they call 'gangsta' masculinities. They asserted that this version of 'bad boy' masculinity did not necessarily lead to anti-education identities but rather that for many of the boys, education and school were only peripheral concerns within their identity constructions. The boys' most powerful identifications were reinforced through popular culture, music and in gendered, classed and racialised relationships in the local area. Archer (2003), drawing on Hesse *et al* (2000), observes that boys' take up and performance of style identities were 'culturally entangled'; in other words, that educational identities are thus also intertwined with, and located in broader cultural and popular discourses of masculinity, race, class, identity and style. She notes that, 'Identities and cultural styles are not distinct, homogenously bounded entities, rather they slip and transgress across fluid and complex phenomena that stretch across different social spheres'.

We saw that cultural styles were important and contested signifiers of local area-based identities and that black cultural forms and particularly musical styles were regarded by most of the boys as superior to 'Asian' forms such as Bollywood. The latter were constructed as feminised and 'typical' as in traditional, and as lacking in cool status. The boys did not identify politically as 'black' through identification with African-Caribbean culture, music or, most significantly, clothes.

Malik, who was already working as an MC during his college course, reported that being Asian was an advantage, as he could take up both black and Asian styles:

> I'm tied to promotion called XXX which is black and, black sort of promotion but I've been approached now by Asian artists or ... have you heard of XXX in Birmingham? I've worked with all Asian promotions during Bhangra night so I do both really. That's the advantage when you're Asian, you can work both sides. I mean on the Asian side you don't see no black Asians, they're very rare or you don't see all Asians around Birmingham...

He suggests that Asians are uniquely positioned to work both sides of a perceived cultural divide and that the rigid divisions the boys identified between 'niggers' and 'teps' is not as evident in the wider region or on the national scene where boundaries are more fluid. He was able to move between and perform a black Asian identity and a Bhangra Asian identity when required for work.

Rapper Tupac Shakur was most commonly cited as the most popular musical artist, though P Diddy, 50cent and Usher were also mentioned. Wasim said he was a fan of white American rap star, Eminem. But other boys were critical of him. Tariq dismissed Eminem mainly because of his lyrical style and specifically the fact that he 'really talks about his mum sometimes and I don't like that'.

Asad, on the other hand, drew on more rigid categorisations of race and culture in his rejection of Eminem:

> Asad: Five to ten years ago you wouldn't see white people dressing the way they do now. If you like from ... you know how people dress ... they don't dress in shirts ... they dress in proper hooded tops and the people, black and Asian they all dress in ... Eminem, he came up and messed everything up. He says one thing, means another. Not like Tupac. If Tupac was alive now he'd probably come and knock Eminem down or something. You know copying ... especially blacks and that ... if you're from their culture ... yeah it's alright to do it. From your own culture instead of taking other people's.
>
> FS: Some people would say that's more like black that's been adapted
>
> Asad: You mean the white people trying to be the blacks?

FS: Who does it belong to?

Asad: Well it's black ...

FS: Who do you mean, black?

Asad: I mean African. When I say Asian, I mean Bengalis, Pakistanis

FS: But you see lots of Asians dressing black

Asad: You can see how people dress. If you see them long enough you'll know the way they dress. If someone's turning round and they've got a hood on you can tell how ... that's a white person or a black person ... but now it's all copying all this about Eminem

FS: That's quite interesting .... Eminem has changed things ... brought hip hop into the mainstream ....

Asad: But he's the only white rapper that's out there and you've got all this heavy metal and he's the only white person rapping away ... so ... you know the white people have got one person and they spend all their money on him and keep him number one and he makes it big time but he's there. If 50cent [and others had been around] then, he wouldn't be as big as he is now would he? It's cos white people have got one of their own to chose

FS: Do you think there could ever be white rapper who's as good as black?

Asad: No cos you can tell ... when the white people rap ... it doesn't sound right. They've got a high voice ... but when black people rap ... They've got that thing to them ... got a deep voice and you can tell. It's good the way they talk. Asian people are more or less the same but the white people ... its all going to change ... they're probably going to bring rock'n'roll and pop into rap

Asad draws here on a range of economic, cultural and racialised arguments and on both cultural and biological notions of race in articulating differences between whites and blacks. For example, he suggests initially that embodied whiteness is easily distinguished from blackness: 'It's the way they move' which suggests performances of, or 'doing' black or white. However he reverts to essential biological notions of race in his discussion of having high or deep voices.

The construction of white, black and Asian hierarchies is also interesting. Blackness is constructed as superior, with Asian occupying the middle rung and whiteness at the bottom. In Asad's construction we see a reversal of the racialised categorisations of Caucasian, Mongoloid and Negroid associated with the doctrine of racial typology (Banton, 1969) or what has since been re-classified as scientific racism.

Asad's account also accepts cultural crossover and multiple identity positioning at the same time as it confirms biological notions of race (black people have deep voices, 'white people can't rap' because their bodies are badly designed). He claims that Asians have a legitimate claim on blackness because they are the same as blacks. White people, on the other hand, lacking any authentic claim to blackness, possess instead economic resources which enable them to successfully market Eminem to a white audience. Without these economic resources and racism in the market he would not be successful. Asad's black separatist, 'every white person is a racist' stance was in part accounted for by the racist assault he had been subjected to. However, it is also significant that black boys were in a minority in both schools and there were no black boys to challenge Asad's and other boys' claims to an authentic black identity.

In observational research of young people in an inner-city London school, Youdell (2003) analysed young people's claims to authenticity in relation to race identities. Black girls consistently rejected a pitch for blackness made by a mixed race Indian and African-Caribbean girl. In the current study, there were few African-Caribbean boys in either of the schools or neighbourhood and they were less numerically significant than the Asian community. There were therefore no challenges to the boys' claims to authentic black identities. In fact the boys consistently reported harmonious relationships across black and Asian communities in their neighbourhoods. After the 2005 Lozells disturbances, however, there was a markedly different mood in the local area. In the research I conducted with girls (reported in Shain, 2010) I found that the divisions between Asian and African-Caribbean communities had become more pronounced.

Conclusion

This chapter has explored the themes of race, nation and culture through the boys' discussion of their sporting and music affiliations which were part of their leisure activities. Although they invested heavily in various local identities, the boys did not take up support of local Oldwych football teams. This seemed to be tied to the need to avoid exclusionary and often violent displays of Englishness which, researchers have argued, constitute working class solidarity, which is now the only thing left for white working class boys (Nayak, 2003). Supporting teams such as Brazil also helped the boys in the study to gain status across peer groups.

Sporting affiliations revealed strong commitment to a 'community' ethos and against individualism. Talk about sport and music was a key mechanism in the working out of divisions and difference within and beyond Muslim categories. The boys' accounts reveal an ongoing process of ordering, fixing and categorising which was central to the construction and negotiation of the boundaries of inclusion and exclusion at local level. These have become significant sources of identity construction where, because of the the declining industrial base in the local area, no work is available.

7

Aspirations, hopes and fears

Introduction

The boys defined schooling primarily with reference to racism and this was a significant factor in the formation of their peer group (see chapter 4). While the boys drew on negative characterisations of schooling, especially in group discussions, they also expressed positive feelings about school, including about teachers and subjects. This chapter reports on their orientations to schooling and 'success' (Bradford and Hey, 2007), their subject preferences and imagined future choices about post 16, career and marriage. I discuss the ways in which subject preferences and career choices relate to school processes such as setting, but also intersect with expectations tied to family and community. In relation to the topic of marriage, we see the boys' mobilisation of Islam to legitimate and defend choices that might otherwise, through cultural and racist discourses, be constructed as illegitimate. The extent to which the boys' choices reflect tradition, community and change within narratives of family and community is assessed.

Orientations to schooling

According to Bradford and Hey (2007), the neo-liberal restructuring of education has resulted in a relentless pursuit of success through policies such as Parental Choice, Beacon and Leading Edge schools, Gifted and Talented and, more recently, Academy and Free Schools. Such polices, initiated by new right conservative governments, have carried through New Labour governments and are embedded in the education policies of the current Coalition government. As Ozga (1999) maintains, these policies are located within a wider framework which ties educa- tion to national competitiveness and sees achievement as the solution to social exclusion. However, rather than equalising opportunities, re- cent analyses (Reay, 2008; Tomlinson, 2008) suggest that these polices have enhanced middle class choice and advantage while reinforcing working class and racialised disadvantage. Policies on citizenship have been designed to help individuals navigate their way through a series of individualised 'personalised' choices, away from the old certainties of class, gender and race communities and class solidarity (Avis, 2006). However, class, race and gender remain salient factors constraining and enabling educational outcomes.

The boys' experiences of schooling were shaped in part by their location in Oldwych which was characterised by disadvantage. A number of schools in the area were identified as 'failing' (see chapter three). In Leyton, success rates in GCSE examinations were low. As in Archer's (2003) study, the boys most commonly talked about school as 'boring but ok', 'alright', 'quite good', though in group discussions they were more likely to say it was 'pants' (Arif and Wahid) and 'really racist' (Arshad) or 'bad'. Their orientations to academic success were similarly mixed and sometimes contradictory. Some boys talked about discard- ing bad boy masculinities to concentrate on work.

Abid was the most academically successful boy at Leyton. As we have seen, his orientation to schooling was a survivalist strategy. He joined in 'boy behaviour' within the safety of a less academic and mixed ability class, where he would not be noticed by the school but would gain status among peers.

Abid:	Yesterday we were [laughs] we were chucking paper around and he just said, 'right that ten minutes detention for you'. [suddenly remembering something] Actually, I didn't go
FS:	You didn't go for your ten minutes?
Abid:	No [laughs]
FS:	What will happen?
Abid:	He's probably going to say something ... 12.35 or something.

Thus Abid was keen to be seen as part of the tough boy peer group and shows no sympathy for the teacher. The interview supported his performance of the idealised Asian masculinity that was valorised by the dominant Asian peer group. But he worked hard to maintain his achievement in more academic subjects, and was confidently on track to pursue a medical career. Here he distinguishes his own orientation to schooling from that of the boys in the lower sets:

Abid:	Typical ... they just don't bother ... all the boys are just one behind me but the girls are like two or three sets behind. They're just dossing around
FS:	What about the girls?
Abid:	I don't know, I don't talk to them
FS:	When they doss around what kinds of things do they do?
Abid:	They talk, throw paper around. I'm ok with my behaviour but I do my work properly

Abid acknowledges that although he occasionally played at being one of the 'tough boys', he made sure that he did his work properly. Aziz was the most socially successful boy but academically was located in the lowest sets. Although he had more or less given up on education for himself – seeing himself as 'just working in a shop' in the future – he did not present as anti-education:

Most of my older brothers have gone college ... good for them they got jobs, and stuff I know one clever guy ... I don't like when people take the Mick. I really like him, he's so clever ... people take on the clever ones ... he's so clever he knows every word in the dictionary I bet you. He's Asian as well. He's one of my best friends and I hope he will be a doctor. (Aziz)

Aziz's account confirms that the clever boys are often targeted for bullying because they choose to follow an academic path. Despite being one of the 'cool' boys, Aziz dissociates himself from such bullying and suggests instead that he has a great deal of respect for these boys who achieve. A number of other boys moved between social success in the peer group and academic success.

Subject likes and dislikes and experiences of the school

My findings on subject preferences concurred with aspects of other recent studies. For example, Francis (2002) found that girls' and boys' choices were not as gender segregated as those in studies conducted in 1990s (see *inter alia*, Thomas, 1990). Thomas found strongly gendered preferences, with boys tending to favour 'harder' scientific subjects and girls 'softer' arts and humanities subjects. In Francis' study (2002), preferences were more diversified and among the most popular boys' subjects were English, maths, science and PE, whilst maths was also ranked high among girls' favoured subjects. Archer (2003) found that Muslim boys in her study showed marked preferences for vocational subjects. She connects this to their classed locations 'in the sense that they privilege practical competencies over more academic text based subjects'(p136). However, they also retained preferences for sciences which, she argues, are strongly gendered.

In my study, choices were more vocationally orientated, with boys showing marked preference for subjects such as Media Studies, Electronics, PE and Design. But these choices were mediated by school definitions of success which were embedded in the practice of setting. Boys in the higher sets tended to show preferences for more traditional academic subjects including maths, science and English, while those in the lower sets showed more vocationally orientated preferences – for design, PE, media and electronics. Among the boys' least favoured subjects were Resistant materials; mathematics especially statistics; RE and English. These likes and dislikes reflect the wider national picture of ethnic minority subject choice in higher education: Muslim students opt for sciences, health, medicine and law over the more traditional academic subjects (Modood, 2006).

The reasons cited for these choices tended to vary according to aspiration and achievement. Higher achieving boys showed more instrumental reasons for their choices:

Farood: Science and maths and IT

FS: Why those?

Farood: Because it's important for my job. I want to be a doctor ... a GP
            First I wanted to be a pilot but my mum said 'no you don't want
            to be a pilot, you want to be a doctor'

Abbas (2004:72) found that middle class students chose subjects on the basis of availability, interest and class orientation. Middle class parents were more likely to take a firmer hold on subject selection and the over-all direction of academic study, while working class Asian parents were less able to direct their children's choices. Farood's family had recently arrived from Afghanistan and although he was reluctant to talk about the circumstances of his arriving to England, his family were by all accounts not middle class. However, his mother, who was raising Farood and his equally high achieving siblings alone, showed middle class aspirations.

Zahid, another relatively high achieving student, expressed intrinsic enjoyment of his subjects as a major reason for choosing them. He said, 'I just like science because different things come up. English is exciting because I like reading and writing'. Conversely, boys in the lower sets were more likely to describe these traditionally academic subjects as 'boring'. They preferred vocational subjects because 'I like the practical elements' (Tariq); 'doing things' (Nadim); 'making things' (Wasim), which were constructed as non-work. Others explicitly stated that they like these subjects because, 'you don't do no work' (Nadim).

Teachers

As in Archer's and Francis's research, teachers were a significant factor in the boys' choices. Abid, a high achiever, placed the emphasis on teachers' ability to teach the subject:

> IT, maths ... depends on teacher. It's not easy, not hard, just ok for me. But the teacher is a bit annoying because he's just covering because our real teacher is pregnant. He's not covering ... things like that real teacher covered more in depth.

Abid suggests here that he is not receiving 'enough knowledge' because his main teacher is absent. Teachers influenced the subject choices of boys located in the middle to lower sets and they emphasised the teacher's personality and ability to control the class rather than their subject knowledge or expertise:

> Rafiq: English ... maths is ok erm statistics ... a bit I don't like that
>   much. RE is just funny cos the teacher starts crying ... he turns
>   around ... paper went into his mouth ... he starts crying

FS:	Poor man
Rafiq:	It's funny
FS:	Is he new?
Rafiq:	Yeah. We've got him every Monday ... but now he has some other teachers with him so we can't do nothing any more. When the other teachers go we just start on him again ...
FS:	Isn't that a bit mean?
Rafiq:	That's funny
FS:	Why is it funny?
Rafiq:	Cos the teachers crying and we're laughing our head off.
FS:	What if someone did it to you? Threw paper at your mouth? How would you react?
Rafiq:	I'd punch em in the face! I wouldn't cry!

Rafiq is saying that the main reason for his dislike of RE is the teacher's inability to control the class. Yet he plays a significant role in preventing that teacher from doing his job. Rafiq feminises the teacher and dissociates himself from the teacher's 'weakness' by saying he would rather retaliate physically than cry, if he were subjected to abuse. The teacher is constructed as weak because he does not stand up to the boys' indiscipline and because he requires the support of others to control his class. This illustrates the power of the peer group and how the need to demonstrate toughness prevented learning in some subjects.

Aziz was one of the most socially successful boys but was defined as academically weak. The Ofsted report for that year had commented on a number of students who had 'simply lost the will to learn' and Aziz was almost certainly among them.

FS:	What about subjects you don't like?
Aziz:	Maths – I don't like the teacher ... he's always shouting at me for no reason. I don't like the teacher
Aziz:	English is so boring. The teacher can't control the lesson and you can't even do no work
FS:	When you say can't control the lesson?
Aziz:	People been talking and the teacher starts shouting and people start laughing at the teacher. She can't control the class

... have to call the head of department. She writes two to three sentences on each page then she talks about half an hour. She tells us the date and title and that's about it and then she talks about half an hour and no-one's listening to her

FS: What does she do when you laugh at her?

Aziz: Nothing that's the thing ... nothing. I feel sorry for her. Cos it's sad isn't it?

Like Rafiq, Aziz points to the teacher's inability to control the class. But wheareas the male teacher was constructed by Rafiq as weak for not standing up for himself, the female teacher is pitied by Aziz. Aziz says he does not join in with tormenting her but nonetheless colludes in the harassment by 'doing nothing'.

Such accounts give a measure of the daily struggles encountered by students and teachers in the attempt to educate the boys. These could be read as assertions of masculine strength and bids for status but the Ofsted reports for both Leyton and Greenbank were peppered with references to classroom indiscipline, a lack of learning and the 'hard' statistics that less than 30 per cent of the students (boys and girls) at Leyton achieved the requisite 5 A*-C grades in that year against a national average of 52 per cent. In Greenbank the figure was only slightly higher at 35 per cent. The high number of fixed-term exclusions and disproportionate ethnic minority exclusion at Greenbank and, to a lesser extent, Leyton were also remarked on in the Ofsted reports for that year.

As well as teachers who could control the class, boys in the lower sets also spoke positively about teachers who were 'nice' and 'kind':

Tariq: Some of them are a bit alright with you

FS: When you say alright, what do you mean?

Tariq: Like some are strict and some are you know like let you do what you want a bit more

FS: To the whole class or just you?

Tarqi: Yeah like to the whole class

FS: Right, so a bit more relaxed

Tariq: Yeah a bit more relaxed

***

Sajid:	Teachers ... [pause] ... I don't like the majority of them. The only one who's good is Mr Pearson and Mr. Waters, he's excellent and er Mrs James.
FS:	What makes these teachers 'good'?
Sajid:	They're always like kind and you know like in conversation like she really gets in there like and you want to say something and she's always there for you miss ... it's just the good thing about the teachers. You want to explain something and they're always there for you miss

Whereas the higher achieving boys emphasised a teacher's ability to teach, the boys in the lower sets placed a premium on the ability of the teacher to 'connect' with them. They were more likely to value a teacher who 'gets in there', and 'is always there for you', invoking again the notions of community and respect discussed in earlier chapters. Nadim mentioned that 'there was only one Jamaican teacher who stick up for me and no one else'.

Post 16 choices

Theories of individualisation, reflexive modernity and the neo-liberalisation of subjectivities (Beck, 1992; Rose, 1996; Giddens, 2001) suggest that traditional social structures such as class, gender and race have lost their significance to people as they navigate their way through their individualised life trajectories. However, other research (Savage, 2000; Skeggs, 2004) suggests that although class, race and gender as, collectively, the foundations of social life may have become less dominant, they remain salient features, constraining or enabling young people's transitions from school to college and university and their life chances (Avis, 2008).

Research on educational outcomes (Mirza, 1992; Gillborn and Mirza, 1998; Gillborn and Youdell, 2000) shows that class and 'race' remain the biggest predictors of educational success and failure. At the same time, however, research on educational choices, particularly in the context of university application (Modood and Shiner, 1994; Modood and Acland, 1998; Ahmad, 2001; Ball et al, 2001; Reay et al, 2002; Abbas, 2004; Modood, 2006; Bhopal, 2010), has consistently shown that despite their less advantaged parental occupations profile, 'most minority ethnic groups were in the 1990s producing greater proportions of applications and admissions to higher education than the rest of the population' (Modood and Acland, 1998:37). Modood (2006) suggests that this trend has continued and Muslim students, often the poorest and most marginalised of English students, are nonetheless more likely than white working class youngsters to submit applications to university.

However, there remains a 'troubling racial divide' (Reay *et al*, 2001; Mirza, 2009) in students' choices, between old and new sectors of higher education. Modood (2006) argues that ethnic minorities are less likely to enter the more prestigious universities, are more likely to drop out and, if they do last the course, they are less likely to get a high grade degree – though all these things apply less to the Indians and Chinese than other minorities. Black groups are more likely to be part time or mature students – which immediately rules them out of the most prestigious high-flying careers that some associate with graduate success. Ethnic minorities are more likely to feature disproportionately in medicine and health related subjects, law and business, engineering and ICT but are under-represented in the pure sciences and the humanities. So only a few universities and not all disciplines can truly claim to be multi-ethnic and, importantly, the universities and courses subscribed to by Muslim students have also been the targets of anti-terror (over)policing. As discussed earlier, Glees and Pope (2005) suggested that individual universities ought to curtail their Muslim student populations as a way of tackling extremism. Some university chancellors have also, in the name of the 'war on terror', volunteered confidential information about Muslim students to counter-terrorist police officers, in the interests of security.

When asked about future educational choices, a minority of the boys said they had not considered their future careers. Nadim said about his exams, 'I don't think about it', while another asked 'what's careers?' (Ibrahim). But most, even those in lower and middle sets, had given consideration to their future choices. Most had career plans and this concurs with the findings of wider research showing that Muslim students aim high (Abbas, 2004) even though they may end up in the less prestigious universities and on less prestigious courses. Among the career choices the boys listed, engineering was most popular, with other choices including electronics, medicine, law and race equality work. Three of the boys wanted to be pilots. Two boys did not know what they wanted to do (Rafiq and Nadim) and Aziz saw himself working in a shop. Two others were already at college (Malik and Arshad) studying business. Sajid and Ibrahim were both working in restaurants near school, and Malik was working the clubs as a DJ during his college course.

These choices contradict dominant policy discourses that suggest that Muslim Asian communities lack aspiration. The boys were located in one of the most materially deprived locations in Oldwych in a school in which racial tensions and the prospects of unemployment were high. Despite being preoccupied with fighting and gaining status through the Asian peer group, the majority of the boys had strong aspirations (McDowell, 2002). For some their careers were not yet well defined, but they were confident that college was the next step. Others talked with confidence and certainty about the higher education course they were planning.

Giving up 'bad boy masculinities' to concentrate on work

A number of the boys who had been in the top or middle sets and also part of the Asian boys' group spoke about leaving 'bad boy' behaviour behind (Archer and Yamashita, 2003) to concentrate on their school work in year 11. One of these was Hamid:

FS: So, which set are you now then?

Hamid: Middle ... I used to be in top yeah but I was naughty and they put me down

FS: Why were you being naughty?

Hamid: 'Cos I got this homework that I couldn't do ... I had difficulties doing it yeah and ... half an hour yeah ... cos I didn't know what to do and I started answering back to the teacher and I swore at her and she like put me down saying I couldn't do the homework ... after that I started being naughty but recently I started behaving and that ... I've got to concentrate now exams are coming up.

Hamid explains here how his 'bad' behaviour had initially started because of a difficult piece of homework which he did not want to admit to being unable to do. This resulted in his being moved down. But he also states that he has made a conscious decision to concentrate on his work and leave behind the 'naughty' behaviour now that exams are approaching. This example also illustrates the impossibility of being socially successful and academically successful at the same time (Youdell, 2008). As in research by Renold (2005), high achieving boys bought into dominant modes of masculinity in not just complicit but also active ways. But they also displayed a working knowledge of when it was necessary to knuckle down to hard work. For the boys who were most successful within the Asian boys' peer group, a career or university was not an option. Aziz, for example, had 'not even thought about it'.

Asad, who had been the subject of a racist attack, had been identified as a high achieving student. But the incident had undermined his confidence and teachers reported being concerned about his progress.

Asad:	I'd say I'm doing quite good – with all this stuff going on. They've been talking about my grades slipping
FS:	You were in the higher sets – I gather from Mrs. James
Asad:	Yeah I have to concentrate on my work. Well before, if they said one thing that made you feel bad ... one little thing will kick off into a big thing. Well, now I'm going to ignore the little things.

FS:	Can I ask you what you see yourself doing in the future?
Asad:	Probably going to university. I was going to be a pilot you know ... but all this ... you know terrorist attack they'd probably get scared shitless ... probably won't work out will it?
FS:	Why not?
Asad:	There are lot of racist people in this world ... you might get another attack or something and I'd get the blame for it – Asians always get the blame. I haven't seen any white person...
FS:	So if you weren't to be pilot?
Asad:	I'll get a mechanics job

Here Asad talks about how his grades had slipped in recent months and vows to leave behind, if only temporarily, the aspects so valued by the Asian boys' peer group. He says he will ignore the 'little things', the mundane racism that is embedded in schooling, and knuckle down to work. However, he also goes on to describe the impact of 9/11 and the

139

'war on terror' on his own imagined future: 'Asians always get the blame'. He says that because of racism he has decided that he will be unable to pursue the career of his choice and has instead opted to downgrade his future career options. His fatalistic attitude is arguably a reflection of his working class location. As I discuss later, other boys also imagined making familiar choices through knowing someone in the trade or through their knowledge of their local area (Nayak, 2003).

'It's too far': staying local

Researchers (Taylor, 1992; Modood and Shiner, 2001; Ball *et al*, 2002: 338) note that a disproportionate number of Asian students apply to home regions. Family and community relations are positively valued and local choices reflect this. Staying at home is a solution to the potential isolation reported by ethnic minority students in their higher education experiences. Archer and Yamashita (2003) found that boys invested heavily in their local identities and could not imagine moving away from their local area for study or work. Reay (2001) too found that working class higher education students talked about geographical constraints. She observed that their transcripts were saturated with a localism that was absent from the narratives of more economically privileged students. Material constraints of travel and finance often mean students are operating within limited spaces, and a few extra stops on the bus or train placed an institution beyond the boundaries of conceivable choice. Ball *et al* found the issue of possibly 'not fitting in' a further constraint on minority students' choices.

Sajid and Asad, who had contacts in London, claimed to be desperate to leave Oldwych. Sajid saw himself going to university elsewhere. Tariq, who wanted to become a medical consultant, also saw himself going to university elsewhere: 'I'd just like to see how it is'. However, in line with the research on working class students, most of the boys expressed highly local choices. A nearby college just two miles from where they lived was considered 'too far' by Aziz:

Aziz:	I'm doing aright
FS:	Which GSCES do you want to do? next year?
Aziz:	No it's this year – Business studies ... Materials and Urdu and statistics, that's a good lesson as well

FS: Will you go to College?

Aziz: Probably Ryton, Camton ... or Tipton ... but it's too far ...

FS: Too far?

Aziz: Yeah it's too far ... I can't be bothered catching a bus in the morning. Ryton's just a walk ...Tipton's too far and I know some people at Ryton

So 'knowing people there' was important. Yet Aziz also talked about moving away from the area in the longer term:

Aziz: It's really boring. I want to move away

FS: Move away? Why?

Aziz: I don't know. I want to move to London

FS: What's in London?

Aziz: I go there a lot ... Near Greenwich

FS: Is it an Asian area?

Aziz: No, quite a lot of Sikhs ... quite a lot of *goray*. In the six weeks holidays I go all the six weeks and every half term. Sometimes I go on the weekends on the train

This is contradictory positioning: the local college is too far away yet Aziz imagines himself leaving the area to live in London. But the one constant is the significance of his existing community or social network. Aziz is prepared to travel to London because of the comfort of an existing network of family and friends. He also has a network of friends at the local college but not at the one further afield.

Discrimination

Dominant policy discourses suggest that Asians tend have low aspirations and that this explains their educational and residential stagnation. Research (eg Abbas, 2004) suggests that Asians tend to aim high but often end up in the new universities on less prestigious courses due to institutional filtering. We saw how Asad had engaged in a process of self exclusion, lowering his expectations because of perceived intuitional racism. Farood also encountered racism – but through his sisters' experiences. Both his older sisters had received top A level grades but had been denied a place at the medical school of their choice, with no formal reason given other than competition. This had influenced

Farood's own aspirations and he had consequently set his sights on a 'lower status university'. Modood (2006) concluded that, all things being equal, a Muslim student is 57 per cent likely to be offered a place at an old university, against 75 per cent of white candidates with similar qualifications.

Family and community role models

Abbas (2004) suggests that the final choices for young South Asian women were strongly influenced by parents, and especially fathers. The boys also reported a number of local influences in respect to their future career choices. For example, Ibrahim's wish to be a car mechanic was influenced by a family member. 'My uncle used to fix cars so like I learned off him so I could do work there ... when I finish school I want to learn more'.

The boys who were most instrumental about subject choices reported that their families' influences were strong. For example, Abids's mother was teaching assistant in a local school and at the time of the research, his sole parent. Farood, too, was in a single parent household at the time, and spoke about his mother in relation to his choice of subjects and career. These experiences to some extent represent feminised choice-making, resonating with research on Asian girls (Mirza, 1992; Bhachu, 1994; Dwyer, 1999; Ahmad, 2001; Abbas, 2004; Bhopal, 2010). This research suggests that mothers played a significant role in nurturing their daughters' ambitions. Zahid talked less about his mother but did acknowledge his sisters as significant role models.

Family and community also played a significant role in Hamid's future choice of career, which centred on youth and race equality work. The older Aziz, who worked in both fields, was a significant role-model for Hamid: 'Er like there's this guy his name's Aziz ... he's my role model'. Zahid also couched his future career in terms of community need and was at pains to say that he is driven by a strong justice ethic and would like to give something back to the community:

> I've always wanted to do Law since I was young and I want to be a barrister or something like that. Go off to Pakistan and help the people who are poor and because what happens in Pakistan is the law's very ... the poor people always get blamed for everything and I don't think that's fair, plus if I went o Pakistan and I killed someone I know I could get away with it ... because I've

got money and I can give ... to everybody ... some poor people can't do that ... so I want to go to Pakistan to help them. (Zahid)

Marriage and families

The issue of marriage within Asian communities has been the focus of media and political debate since the 1970s, when stories of runaway brides and honour killings over escaped or forced marriages dominated public discourses on Asian families. Theories of risk and reflexive modernity stress the individualised nature of biographies and choices in late modernity. However, dominant discourses on marriage within Asian and Muslim communities as espoused, for example, by the then Home Secretary David Blunkett in the aftermath of the 2001 distur-bances in England, position them as overly determined by culture and religious practices.

In relation to schooling, research (Brah and Minhas, 1986; Parmar, 1988; Dwyer, 1999; Shain, 2003) has challenged academic accounts that posi-tioned Asian youth, especially girls, as caught between two cultures and facing a future of forced traditional marriage. These researchers suggest instead that racist assumptions about Pakistani and Bangladeshi com-munities are often embedded in schools through teachers' and careers officers' assumptions that Asian girls would end up having arranged marriages so did not need schooling (Parmar, 1988). A Foreign and Com-monwealth Office-commissioned report (Eade and Samad, 2002) found that parents' class and educational background are closely tied to the amount of choice children are offered. In the aftermath of the July 2005 bombings and through discourses on the 'war on terror', arguments about arranged (often used interchangeably with forced) marriages have also been used to justify intense policing of Muslim communities (Wilson, 2006; Bhopal, 2010).

In my earlier research (Shain, 2003), I found that girls expressed a range of views about arranged marriage. The girls most likely to defend tradi-tional arranged marriages were those who were in the lower sets and who experienced the most severe racism in school. Girls in the mid to higher sets were more confident about being able to negotiate their future choice of partner but expected to marry someone of the same ethnic background.

The boys in the current study had a lot to say about arranged marriages but virtually all of them disagreed with the idea of arranged marriages when talking about their own futures. Only one boy, Yasser, who described himself as mixed race Pakistani and white English, defended the practice of arranged marriage 'Because you want people from your family'. Yasser had an issue about belonging. He was the only mixed-race boy and he attended a different 'successful school' (a Catholic school) to the other boys. His attendance at the youth group was a rare opportunity for him to mix with Muslims and his need to fit in with the other boys and prove his Pakistani credentials was possibly a factor in his defence of arranged marriages.

While disagreeing with the idea, Rafiq said he would consider going along with an arranged marriage, 'because parents look after us for how long and they give me whatever I want. So I don't know'. However, Malik appeared to draw on discourses of cultural pathology when he talked about a 'backward mentality' among Asian communities:

Malik: What I'm saying is that there's this backward mentality ... you've got to recognise that you can't force your children to spend their lives because at the end of the day it's the next person's life yeah, and from the Islamic point of view, we've all got to understand that as long as they're Muslims and they accept the Sharia like you do, well there would be problem there. Ok your mum and dad do get a say in it but they should just be happy with you ... because that doesn't resolve nothing. I mean if I was to send my friend Nadim here and not bring him back until he's married ... and if he's not happy ...Then what's the point?

Mushtaq: He might come back hating you

FS: Is there anyone here who could see themselves marrying a non-Muslim?

Nadim: Omer ... he's got a ...

Omer: I would marry her but I would turn her into a Muslim

Nadim: His mum will say to him ...

Malik: ... If you marry a non-Muslim and you want children with a non-Muslim then those children are classed as *haraam* anyway

BG: How many of you believe that?

           ***

Sajid: Yeah because you marry someone who you don't know and it's not just fair because really you should be picking yourself not your mum and dad. Because how you know it's going to work out fine?

Malik initially draws on a discourse of tradition, suggesting there is backward mentality among Asian communities which leads them to force their children to marry against their will. However, he then goes on to draw on Islamic discourse to argue that change is not permitted, that having mixed race children is against Sharia law. Later, he contrasts the 'backward mentality' with his own experience of being allowed to travel freely and being trusted, so challenging the idea that all Muslim families are constrained by such a 'mentality' or repression. But the gender specificity of his response needs to be acknowledged: it is not clear whether this freedom is or should, in Malik's view, be applied equally to girls.

> My parents, on the whole yeah, my parents are chillin'. Well not chillin, because at the end of the day, yeah, I'm out and about MC'ing in all clubs all over the country and now my mum won't say this that bla, bla, bla, she'll say mate go out do it. But she knows that I won't drink and I won't bring a girl home and have a kid before I'm married. Because these are the sort the things that basically we've been brought up that you don't do. So my mum assumes that it's safe for me to go out ... so ... (Malik)

The boys talked positively about their families and defended them. In some cases the boys suggested that older generations were more re-laxed and lenient than the boys were. 'As far as these two go, their dad's more chilled out than them two' (Malik). Mudasser's father was also described as 'chilled'. For example, Arshad commented on the freedom given to Mudasser: 'his dad is trying to tell us yeah, that son, this is what there is, as long as you choose that way you can choose that way but at the end of the day this is what their life it is'. (Arshad)

Family and tradition were cited by the boys as significant factors in their future decisions about marriage. However, as Abid's and other accounts suggest, the boys' choices did not reflect fixed traditions. Their ex-pressed preferences reflected not only change in their narratives but also a greater degree of integration into western society than currently suggested by dominant discourses on Muslim and Asian families.

Abid: Er this sounds a bit funny but ... I want to get married before my grandparents pass on

FS: What kind of person would that have to be?

Abid: Muslim ... not sure yet. I'm too young to think about that sort of stuff.

FS: But would you marry an English person?

Abid: I don't know maybe ... don't really matter as long as they're Muslim

***

Sajid: I'd marry someone who I know. I don't want an arranged marriage. I'd prefer a love marriage

FS: Would you marry an English girl?

Sajid: Would I? It depends really miss. If I've known her for a long time but it depends on the parents

The boys expressed a range of views about their families on marriage. They were far more confident about their own agency in choices than the Muslim and Asian girls in my research, who, although confident, reported having to work hard at persuading parents to accept the role of education in their future. The majority of the girls expected the family to have a significant role in the decision, and lower achieving girls expected families to choose. In the current study, boys took it for granted they would have a choice.

Asad: Well I've had a bit of a chat with my parents anyway ... and they said we won't force you to do anything you don't want to do. So if you don't want to marry the person we choose you can marry someone else. If you've found someone you tell us and we'll see. So they're quite good about it. You see the people round here ... I got a choice so that's alright

What 'sort' of girl?

All the boys discussed their identities within a heterosexual context, as in Archer's study (2003:102). The Muslim boys Archer interviewed expected their families to be involved in their decisions about future marriages. Archer found that boys were more likely to frame their rejection of such marriages within a macho misogynistic discourse, for example, that focused on the 'quality' of woman they might marry rather than in moral terms. One boy expressed a worry that his future bride could be 'spotty' (*ibid*:103).

For Asad, it was important that his future wife was not 'typical', but more important still was his preference for 'pure' Bengali children:

> She can't be typical – she has to have, y'know an education. Not a degree. As long as she can speak English properly ... good common sense, she knows right from wrong ... it's good enough for me.

> I don't really mind where they're from but it would just be better if she was from the same background so kids can be 100 per cent Bengali. (Asad)

Aziz, like Asad, invoked notions of 'tepness' by suggesting that his future wife should be able to stand up for herself. 'A chilled out person basically ... If they're like boring ... do whatever I say then I don't think I'll really like em'. That is, not be too passive, a quality often associated by the boys with girls who were brought over from Pakistan or Bangladesh.

Sajid considered looks and personality to be important in a future wife:

Sajid:	Can I just go back to that marriage thing like ... you know my mum she keeps on like guiding me about you know. I know a few girls from Pakistan, she keeps on like showing me photos ... do you want to marry her? I'm like, No I'm alright
FS:	A bit of pressure there then?
Sajid:	I know she keeps ...
FS:	Are they cousins?
Sajid:	Cousins and friends really. There's this really dark one Miss. I just do not like her face. My mum keeps on showing it me
FS:	Why, because she's dark?
Sajid:	She's ugly *and* dark [laughs]
FS:	But what if she's a nice person?
Sajid:	I don't care. At the end of the day all I'm looking for is looks and personality miss and the way she talks to other people – if she's got respect for other people that's alright

Sajid talks openly about not wanting someone with dark skin. This stems from a colonial legacy when white-skinned people had higher status and power and also resonates with biological notions of racism which were institutionalised through colonial discourses during Empire. Dark skin was commonly associated with labour and work in the sun. White skin carries the colonial notion of power and superiority. Whole industries have developed on the back of these racialised categorisations in the Indian subcontinent (Shankar and Subish, 2007). The superiority of white skin is also reflected in the Indian film industry and carried through into British catalogues for Asian clothing. *Suits me* and *Rupali* employ white-skinned girls and even use white English child models to sell traditional Indian clothes. The massive industry in skin lightening creams exploits the preference for white skin. In the 1800s very white skin was deemed desirable by many people of European descent – women reportedly even ate arsenic to make their skins paler.

'It's ok to marry a white girl'

A number of boys saw themselves marrying English girls and Islam was drawn on to justify these choices. Even Zahid, who distanced himself from 'western' habits of drinking and going out, said he would marry an English girl and drew on a discourse of Islam to defend his choice.

Zahid:	It's not in Islam ... in the Quran or *Hadith*, it says nothing, in the religion says that ... love marriage .... If someone loves someone I believe they should get married no matter what they are because people nowadays are after *Choudhurys* and *Rajas* you know all these and I think that's a bit pathetic, and that's not in our religion any way. People talk things about *Isla* but they don't realise they're making a big issue of it. If someone loves someone they should just get married. (Zahid)
FS:	So do you see yourself getting married in a few years? What kind of a person would that be then?
Zahid:	Basically I don't know like ... what like my parents views is, my mother's, and its not necessary that I'll listen to them. If it feels wrong
FS:	Would you marry someone who is not a Muslim?
Zahid:	Yeah, if they turned to Muslim
FS:	Ok ... so they could be English?

Zahid: In our religion it's very big *Suwab* if you make someone into a Muslim

FS: What about of girls? Is it ok for them to do it too?

Zahid: Yeah. Girls and boys. Like nowadays people a make a big issue that girls can't go to college, they can't do this, can't go out. But erm, it is wrong for them to go out and do bad things you know against their religion but they can always go to college to get their education ... education doesn't do harm at all. Because my sister. My older sister she couldn't do her GCSEs because she was ill and the doctor said she couldn't do them so that was the reason otherwise she was alright. She's going to college next September *inshallah*. But I know some people who say they are at college they going to be like this or that. They just ruin their lives aren't they, by doing that?

FS: Doing what?

Zahid: Like having boyfriends

Zahid asserts that there is no law in Islam preventing Muslims from making their own choice in relation to marriage and that converting a future spouse to Islam earns *Suwab* (God's blessing). But he strategically avoids the questions of whether this blessing would be equally applied to girls. He says girls have an equal right to be educated, as his own sisters have been, but only as long as they behave modestly and avoid romantic relationships. If they do not and are removed from college, they only have themselves to blame. Zahid is drawing on what Hopkins calls a discourse of sexist equality (Hopkins, 2005), suggesting that girls and women are equal but also displaying double standards around sex and relationships.

Other boys also suggested that marrying a non-Muslim was not only permissible but particularly condoned within Islam. Asad for example said, 'Being Muslim ... cos when you're Muslim, you don't think about she's a white person, I won't marry her. As long as you like her ... if you turn her into Muslim that's good enough for Islam'. Arif drew on a religious discourse to legitimate his potential choice of a non-Muslim future wife. Wahid draws on a discourse of integration to justify his own future preference:

Arif: Well it depends on the situation. In our religion you've got to impress your parents ... if you impress your parents then Allah

149

> will be pleased with you and you've more chance of going to paradise

Wahid: I'm not bothered what the background is as long as they're Muslim ... better if they're not cos then you can be more mixed. You see parents say you have to marry what they are [somebody of the same culture/faith]

Hamid was one of the few boys who talked openly about having a relationship with a white English girl. He talked about it in the past tense but notably without the disrespect for white girls that politicians Jack Straw and Ann Cryer claim was inherently a Pakistani cultural trait.

Hamid: I don't really like it [arranged marriages] cos I don't like ... but you can have your own choice ... if you don't like em then you don't have to get married but usually some people force their children to get married ... I don't know, I used to have a girlfriend and my mum knew about it and used to tell me that you shouldn't marry English girls

FS: Was it an English girl?

Hamid: Yeah, she used to tell me and stuff ... lecture and that

FS: How did you react to that?

Hamid: I just started arguing

FS: So you can see yourself marrying an English woman – she wouldn't have to be a Muslim?

Hamid: No that's the thing, right, she would have to be a Muslim. I'd have to bring to into Muslim

FS: Would that be for yourself or for your family?

Hamid: For my family ... otherwise I couldn't get married to her

FS: But it wouldn't matter to you?

Hamid: No

Like the other Leyton boys, Hamid claims that he would marry a non Muslim but would 'covert her' to Islam. However, unlike the boys who cited Islamic discourses to justify their possible preferences for non Muslims, Hamid is clear about the fact that this would be a compromise for his family. Such accounts suggest the continued significance of the family in future choices, but at the same time, significant change too, in the boys' suggestions that they might consider, and even fight for, non

Muslim spouses. They also represent a challenge to the provocative statements made by politicians about Muslim boys' apparent lack of respect for white girls. The boys clearly did not see them as 'easy meat' (Straw, 2010) but as potential long term partners. In a number of cases they signalled their willingness to challenge traditional expectations in support of their choices.

Conclusion

This chapter considered the boys' subject preferences and their future aspirations in terms of both education and personal relationships. Most of the boys showed marked preferences for vocational subjects in their post 16 studies. This concurs with wider research and statistical evidence on the choices made by Muslim and ethnic minority students. Boys in the higher sets were more instrumental and determined about their future educational paths and more likely to opt for careers in medicine or law. However, virtually all expressed a strong desire to continue their studies after compulsory schooling. One of the factors to be considered here is the absence of employment directly after completing schooling, unlike the old transition from schooling to manual labour. Brine (2005) observes that through lifelong learning, the state has managed to contain potentially dangerous populations of young working class men with no prospect of work.

As we find in wider research on working class students, the need to stay in their own neighbourhood was a strong constraining factor, though some boys talked confidently about moving away from the local area. Contrary to theories suggesting that individual biographies are tied less to tradition and social structures of class, race and gender, the boys' choices reflected strong ties with community and tradition. The boys imagined a heterosexual future and expected to have a strong say in their future choice of marriage. They drew on religion to legitimate and defend choices that might otherwise have been considered unacceptable. These choices reflected both tradition and change, so presenting a challenge both to dominant policy and political discourses which regard Muslim communities to be overly determined by narratives of tradition and culture, and individualisation theories which suggest that young people's choices are increasingly becoming less influenced by tradition and social structures of class, race and gender.

8

Conclusion

Muslim boys have come to occupy the role of new folk devils at a time of significant economic, political and cultural global change. Their emergence as folk devils is located in the wider global shifts marked by the end of Cold War politics and the 'turn to religion', which has seen Islam emerge as a new, global enemy. In Britain, the manufacturing base that attracted immigrant workers in the 1960s to settle in industrial towns and cities declined significantly, causing widespread unemployment and accompanying disadvantage in educational and labour markets for the later generations.

The 'war on terror', the ideological justification for the US neo-conservative project for an American century (Harvey, 2003), has significantly affected Muslim communities in the West. In Britain, the Pakistani and Bangladeshi communities – already among the most disadvantaged of ethnic minority communities – have been subject to intense scrutiny and surveillance in the debates about the limits of multiculturalism. These debates have been particularly heated since the inner city disturbances in 2001 and the London transport bombings in 2005. Muslim boys have emerged as symbols of crisis and change against this backdrop, and arguments about their supposed underachievement in the educational and labour market have been used to underscore dominant discourses of dangerous and violent masculinity.

As Alexander (2000, 2004) has argued, young people from Pakistani and Bangladeshi communities are positioned as the products of a backward culture and at the same time as functioning outside of that culture.

They are the embodiment of its myriad failures. In contrast to these dominant discourses, the accounts presented in this book illustrate a range of preoccupations that influence and shape the identities of the boys. The conclusions can be summarised around four key themes.

Social and political identifications

Contrary to current political and policy discourses which position young people as disinterested and lacking knowledge about politics, the boys in this study expressed strong opinions on global, national and local politics. This indicates an active engagement with political issues. The boys adopted a range of strategies to actively counter dominant discourses on the 'war on terror' that position Muslims as extremists or harbourers of terrorists. The majority of the boys self-defined as Muslims and asserted strong collective Muslim masculinities to counter anti-Muslim racism in their local contexts. These strong collective Muslim masculinities were discursively constructed by the boys as superior to the perceived individualism of western European, white norms and family practices. Such assertions often met with further stigmatisation by their peers.

These identities were not fixed, however. In the context of schooling and peer relations, an alternative Asian masculinity was constructed in opposition to what was perceived by the boys as the white, racist and imperialist culture of the school. Racialised Asian masculine identities were constructed externally, by a collective stigmatising of Muslim Asian boys as trouble-makers and gang members or sometimes simply as Muslims. Internally, a range of cultural resources were drawn on to gain or refuse membership. However, successful performances of Asian masculinity were read against the dominant discourses of the school as failed academic identities. While some boys such as Abid and Asad managed strategically to work both social and academic identities, for the boys in the lower sets, strong investments in hegemonic Asian masculinity impacted negatively on academic achievement.

Their local neighbourhood identifications also reveal complexity. The boys' investments in local area identities were sometimes racialised but, at other times, these area-based identifications cross-cut ethnic, racial and religious identities. We saw that these neighbourhood struggles intersected with local histories in Oldwych: the white working class struggles over territory and space which were once contested in the same geographical space, and also the antiracist struggles once mobilised around work and the unions. In the current economic climate where work is no longer a main source of identity, the boys' struggles over ownership and belonging in relation to the local area could be read to offer new cultural resources for collective identity formation. Identifications with neighbourhood had the effect of reinforcing a working class localism which produced what might, through discourses of self-segregation, be perceived as residential stagnation. However, in most cases, their decisions to stay local were based pragmatically on their need for support networks in the face of discrimination. Fierce struggles in defence of neighbourhoods, including from threat of racist attack, sometimes reinforced discourses of violent Muslim masculinity.

Sporting affiliations revealed classed commitments to a community ethos and a rejection of individualism. However, these were also complex and contradictory at times, with boys explicitly rejecting Englishness through their expressed lack of support of local and national English football teams. Their preferences for England over Germany, however, revealed the 'Englishness' of the boys.

The boys' accounts reveal an ongoing process of ordering, fixing and categorising, which appears to be central to the working out of difference at the local level and to the construction of racialised gendered collective identities in new times. This identity work confirms the schools as key spaces and locations where discourses may be challenged or reinforced and where issues of belonging, inclusion and exclusion are struggled with and contested on a daily basis.

Change and tradition

A second key theme relates to the extent to which the boys' strategic responses represent change or tradition. As I have suggested, theories of risk, reflexive modernisation and the neo-liberal subjectivities (Beck, 1992; Rose,1996; Giddens, 2000;) suggest that choices and lifestyles and biographies are increasingly becoming detached from the local bonds of tradition that were once central in their production. It is posited that the traditional structures of place, class, race and gender no longer have the same hold on, and meaning to, individuals that they once did. However, dominant culturalist readings of Muslim communities position them as extremely tradition-bound, insular and incapable of change. I have argued that dominant narratives of Muslim communities represent them as too tradition-bound to be capable of changing.

The boys' accounts suggest that traditional structures of class, gender, ethnicity and neighbourhood remain highly significant in their construction of current and future choices and life trajectories. They fiercely defended local identities and placed a strong emphasis on loyalty, backup and 'being there' for friends and family. Such constructions also reinforced masculine discourses, particularly through notions of 'protecting' girls. Struggles over territory and turf reinforced traditional gender boundaries and supported the masculine colonisation of public space. These struggles differentially positioned white and Asian girls as respectively predatory and in need of protection, but collectively as symbols of masculinity. The boys' talk about marriage reflected both change *and* tradition. Families were constructed as central to future choices. However, the boys also displayed confidence in their ability to change their parents' expectations, drawing on religious discourse to support their 'changed' preference and choices for non-Muslim girls as future spouses. Such talk challenged both the thesis of individualisation and fixed and static conceptions of cultures that are embedded in discourses of self-segregation.

Teaching, Britishness and Empire

The third major implication of the research relates to schooling in a post 9/11 context. The boys' accounts suggested an intense atmosphere in the immediate aftermath of the event. The research took place before the July 2005 London bombings – but one might expect an even more charged atmosphere in schools thereafter. The boys reported positive attempts to deal with the immediate fallout of the 2001 events in their schools, including one incident in which a normal history lesson was abandoned in response to a throw-away comment made by two of the boys (chapter three). Hamid and one of his friends suggested to the teacher 'for a joke' that they would join the Taliban after leaving school. In the racially charged atmosphere of schooling at the time, the comment was quite likely more than a joke. It was probably a bid for status among the peer group and at the same time a challenge to the authority represented by the teacher.

The teacher's response was appreciated by the boys because it enabled an in-depth discussion of the issues. This is not to suggest that other teachers in the school did not attempt to tackle the issue through their teaching – the boys reported other individual and sympathetic attempts to deal with the impact of the 'war on terror'. They also reported assemblies aimed at calming the atmosphere in the immediate aftermath of the 9/11 attacks. But the boys reported a lack of curricular engagement by their schools with issues raised by the 'war on terror'. They reported feeling marginalised by attempts at peace-building and their accounts suggested an institutionalisation of a particular narrative of British/US superiority in the 'war on terror'. Citizenship classes had only recently been introduced and had not yet made any impact on the boys.

Consequently, the proposed revisions to the history curriculum are particularly significant. The teaching of the British history of empire through the curriculum could, if approached with sensitivity, clarity and historical rigour, be a significant space for challenging some of the historical underpinnings of current discourses that position Muslims as heathen or backward and black groups as inferior, different or barbaric. It could be a way of drawing out commonalities between racialised sections of the working class through learning about the colonial forces that brought Muslim communities to settle in Britain and the contributions they made to rebuilding Britain after the Second World War.

However, the proposed changes need to be read in the context of wider economic, political and ideological factors that inspire the need for a narrative re-telling of Britain's 'island story'. One such may be what Gilroy (2004) refers to as 'postcolonial melancholia' in the face of Britain's declining imperial and economic power. As discussed in chapter one, patriotic appeals to a 'British spirit' were made by David Cameron in his first Conservative party speech as Prime Minister in October 2010. The Union Jack flag was prominently displayed behind him as significant cuts to public funding were announced, yet the cuts themselves were justified through discourses of 'choice' and 'fairness' that ideologically target and differentiate as 'unBritish' those who, for example, have large families, are welfare dependent, or long term unemployed.

On the same day, the end to universal child benefit was defended by the Culture Secretary through a discourse of choice. In an interview broadcast on *Newsnight* (October 5, 2010), he urged larger families to take the consequences for their choices and accept reduced government support. These and other measures, including the ending of the Educational Maintenance Allowance, target (albeit indirectly) working class Muslim and Asian families, who are more likely to be dependent on state benefits because of economic location, racial discrimination in labour and educational markets.

Race and racism

The boys' accounts of schooling and neighbourhood relations reveal the complex and contradictory nature of contemporary racism – the fourth factor. On the one hand the boys report being addressed as *terrorists* and *Bin Laden*, which illustrates how the politicisation and racialisation of religion shape contemporary racist discourse. Yet biological notions of race were drawn on by the boys themselves in everyday encounters. Asad, for example, remarked that ' white men can't rap' because their bodies are not designed for it.

As Hall (1980) observes, contemporary racism contains variants of old themes and draws on a range of discourses about inferiority and superiority, biology, culture and difference. Some of the ideas and images present in current discourses on Muslim masculinity re-work old colonial notions such as the backwardness and barbarity of Muslim cultures. Discourses of extremism and terrorism also plug into, but re-work, colonial stereotypes about Muslims as sly, untrustworthy and as ruthless and dangerous.

Themes of race, culture and nation were also evident in the sifting, sorting and ordering of bodies, choices and preferences as part of ongoing struggles over belonging, inclusion and exclusion. Although the boys explicitly rejected Englishness and Britishness in their self-definitions, and often positioned themselves in opposition to the Britishness represented through the global 'war on terror', and national political discourses and debates, they also, through their school and neighbourhood relations, made strong claims on Britishness and even Englishness, which they expressed in their affiliations and their futures choices. All of this supports Amin's (2002) observation:

There is a complexity to the cultural identity of Asian youth that cannot be re-duced to the stereotype of traditional Muslim, Hindu, Sikh lives, to the bad masculinities of gang life ... to the all too frequently repeated idea of their entrapment between two cultures ...Their frustration and public anger cannot be detached from their identities as a new generation of British Asians claim-ing in full the right to belong to [their local neighbourhoods] *and* the nation, but whose Britishness includes Islam, *halal* meat, family honour and cultural resources located in diaspora networks. (Amin, 2002:10)

References

Abbas, T (2004) *The Education of British South Asians*. London: PalgraveMacmillan

Abbas, T (2005) (Ed) *Muslim Britain: Communities Under Pressure*. London: Zed Books

Abbas, T (2007) (Ed) *Islamic Political Radicalism*. Edinburgh: Edinburgh University Press

Abrams, M (1959) *The Teenage Consumer*. London: Routledge and Kegan Paul

Ahmad, F (2001) 'Modern Traditions? British Muslim Women and Academic Achievement'. *Gender and Education* 13(2):137-152

Alexander, C (1996) *The Art of Being Black*. Buckingham: Open University Press

Alexander, C (2000) *The Asian Gang*. Oxford: Berg

Alexander, C (2004) Imagining the Asian Gang: ethnicity, masculinity, and youth after 'the riots'. *Critical Social Policy*, 24(4):526-549

Amin, A (2002) Ethnicity and the multicultural city: living with diversity, *Environment and Planning A* 34(6): 959-980

Amos, V and Parmar, P (1981) Resistances and responses: the experiences of black girls in Britain, in A McRobbie and T McCabe (Eds) *Feminism for Girls: An Adventure Story*. London: Routledge and Kegan Paul

Amos, V and Parmar, P (1984) Challenging imperial feminism. *Feminist Review* (23): 31-57

Ansari, H (2004) *'The Infidel Within': Muslims in Britain since 1800*. London: Hurst

Ansell, A E (1997) *New Right, New Racism: Race and Reaction in the United States and Britain*. London: Macmillan

Anthias, F and Yuval-Davis, N (1992) *Racialized Boundaries*. London: Routledge and Kegan Paul

Anwar, M (1979) *The Myth of Return: Pakistanis in Britain*. London: Heinemann

Anwar, M (1986) *Race and Politics: Ethnic Minorities and the British Political System*. London: Tavistock Publications.

Anyon, J (1983) Intersections of gender and class: accommodation and resistance by working class and affluent females to contradictory sex-role ideologies, in S Walker and L Barton (Eds) *Gender, Class and Education*. London: Croom Helm

Apple, M (1999) The absent presence of race in education. *Race, Ethnicity and Education*, 2 (1): 9-16

Archer, L (2003) *Race, Masculinity and Schooling: Muslim boys and Education.* Buckingham: Open University Press

Archer, L and Francis, B (2007) *Understanding Minority Ethnic Achievement: the role of race, class, gender and 'success'.* London: Routledge

Archer, L and Yamashita, H (2003) Theorising Inner-city Masculinities: 'race', class, gender and education. *Gender and Education*, 15(2):115-132

Avis, J (2008) Class, economism, individualisation and post compulsory education and training. *Journal for Critical Education Policy Studies*, 6(2):37-53

Back, L (1994) The sounds of the city. *Anthropology in Action*, 1(1):11-16

Back, L, Crabbe, T, Solomos, J (2000) *The Changing Face of Football: Racism, Identity and Multicuture in the English Game.* Oxford: Berg

Back, L, Keith, M, Khan, A, Shukra, K, Solomos, J (2002) The Return of Assimilationism: Race, Multiculturalism and New Labour. *Sociological Research Online*, vol. 7, no. 2, <http://www.socresonline.org.uk/7/2/back.html

Bagguley P and Hussain, Y (2005) Flying the flag for England? Citizenship, religion and cultural identity among British Pakistani Muslims, in T Abbas (Ed) *Muslim Britain: communities under Pressure.* London: Zed Books

Bagguley, P and Hussain, Y (2008) *Riotous Citizens: ethnic conflict in multicultural Britain.* Aldershot: Ashgate

Bains, H (1988) Southall youth: an old-fashioned story, in P Cohen and H Bains (Eds), *Multi-Racist Britain.* London: MacMillan

Ball, S (1990) *Politics and Policy Making in Education.* London: Routledge

Ball S, Davies J, David M, Reay D (2002) 'Classification' and 'judgement': social class and the 'cognitive structures' of choice of higher education. *British Journal of Sociology* 23(1)51-72

Barker, M (1981) *The New Racism.* London: Junction Books

Basit, T (1997) *Eastern Values, Western Milieu: Identities and Aspirations of Adolescent British Muslim Girl.* Aldershot: Ashgate

Beck, Ulrich (1992) *Risk Society: Towards a New Modernity.* London: Sage

Beck, U and Beck-Gernsheim, E (2002) *Individualization: Institutionalized Individualism and its Social and Political Consequences.* London: Sage

Beckerlegge, G (1991). 'Strong cultures' and discrete religions: the influence of imperialism. *New Community* 17(2):201-210

Bennett, A (1999) Subcultures or neo-tribes? Rethinking the relationship between youth, style and musical taste. *Sociology* 33(3):599-617

Bepplar Spahl, S (2010) Thilo Sarrazin: the dark side of multiculturalism. *Spiked*, 13 September, available at http://www.spiked-online.com/index.php/site/article/9549/ accessed October 10, 2010

Bhachu, P (1991) Culture and ethnicity amongst Punjabi Sikh women in 1990s Britain. *New Community* 17(3):401-412

Bhavnani, K (1993) Towards a multicultural Europe?: 'Race', nation and identity in 1992 and beyond. *Feminist Review* (45):30-45

Bhavnani, K (1994) *Talking Politics: A Psychological Framing of Views from Youth in Britain.* Cambridge:Cambridge Unviersity Press

Bhavnani, K and Phoenix, A (1995) Identities and Racisms: differences and commonalities, *Feminism Psychology.* 5(2)294-298

Bhopal, K (2010) *Asian Women and Higher Education: communities of practice.* Stoke-on-Trent: Trentham

Blair, T (1997) PM speech on 'Bringing Britain together', South London 8 December, 1997

Blair, T (2004) Resignation announcement speech, 2 May, BBC

Blair, T (2005) Statement from Downing Street on the 2005 bomb blasts, available at http://news.bbc.co.uk/1/hi/uk/4659953.stm accessed 31 August, 2009

Blair, T (2006) The duty to integrate; speech delivered 7 December, available at http://news.bbc.co.uk/1/hi/uk_politics/6219626.stm accessed 31 August, 2009

Blears, H (2009) Many Voices: understanding the debate about preventing violent extremism lecture delivered to London School of Economics, 25 February, available at http://www2.lse.ac.uk/publicEvents/events/2008/20081203t1539z001.aspx#generated-subheading2 accessed 31 August, 2009

Blunkett, D (2001) Blunkett's 'British test' for immigrants. *Independent.co.uk*, December 9 available at http://www.independent.co.uk/news/uk/politics/blunketts-british-test-for-immigrants-619629.html accessed 31 August, 2009

Blunkett, D (2003) Blunkett dumps 'institutional racism', *Guardian*, 14 January http://www.guardian.co.uk/politics/2003/jan/14/immigrationpolicy.race accessed 31 August, 2010

Bottero, W (2009) Class in the 21st Century, in K Sveinsson, (Ed), *Who cares about the white working class.* London: Runneymede Bulletin

Bourdieu, P (1978) Sport and social class. *Social Science information* 17(6) 819-840

Bourdieu, P (1986) *Distinction: A Social Critique of the Judgement of Taste.* London: Routledge

Bourdieu, P and Passeron, J C (1977) *Reproduction in education, society and culture.* London: Sage

Bracchi, P (2009) Classroom apartheid: teachers who were afraid to discipline thuggish minority of Asian pupils for fear of being branded racist. *Mail Online*, 30 October http://www.dailymail.co.uk/news/article-1223938/The-classroom-apartheid-teachers-frightened-discipline-thuggish-minority-Asian-pupils-fear-branded-racist.html accessed 30 October, 2009

Bradford, S. and Hey, V. (2007) Successful Subjectivities? The successification of Class, Ethnic and Gender Positions, *Journal of Education Policy*, 22, (6): 595-614

163

Brah, A (1993) Reframing Europe: en-gendered racisms, ethnicities and nationalisms in contemporary Western Europe. *Feminist Review* (43):9-28

Brah, A (1992) Difference. diversity and differentiation, in J Donald, and A Rattansi (Eds) Race, Culture and Difference. London: Open University in association with Sage

Brah, A (1994) Time, place and others: discourses of race, nation and ethnicity. *Sociology* 28(3):805-13

Brah, A (1996) *Cartogrophies of Diaspora*. London: Routledge

Brah, A and Minhas, R (1985) Structural racism or cultural difference, in G Weiner (Ed) *Just a Bunch of Girls*. Buckingham: Open University Press

Brine, J (2006) Lifelong learning and the knowledge economy: those that know and those that do not-the discourse of the European Union. *British Educational Research Journal*, 32(5):649-665

Brown, G (2004) speech at the British Council lectures, given 7 July http://www.guardian.co.uk/politics/2004/jul/08/uk.lbour accessed 31 August, 2010

Brown, G (2006) Britishness speech given to the Commonwealth Club, London http://www.guardian.co.uk/politics/2007/feb/27/immigrationpolicy.race accessed 31 August, 2010

Brown, G (2008) The mission of our times; the fair society speech given to the Labour Party conference, 22 September, available at http://www2.labour.org.uk/gordon_brown_conference accessed 31 August, 2010

Buijs, F J, Demant, F and Hamdy, A (2006) *Strijders van eigen bodem. Radicale en democratische moslims in Nederland*. Amsterdam: University Press

Burdsey, D (2006) No balls games allowed A Socio-Historical Examination of the Development and Social Significance of British Asian Football Clubs. *Journal of Ethnic and Migration Studies* 32(3):477-496

Burdsey, D (2007) Role with the punches: the construction and representation of Amir Khan as a role model for multiethnic Britain. *Sociological Review* 55:611-631

Burnett, J (2009) Racism and the state: authoritarianism and coercion' in R Coleman, J Sim, S Tombs, and D Whyte (Eds) *State, Power, Crime*. London: Sage

Cain, M (1986) Realism, feminism, methodology and the law. *International Journal of Sociology of Law*, 14(3-4): 255-267

Cambell, H (1980) Rasatafari – culture of resistance. *Race and Class* xxii(1):1-23

Campaign Against Racism and Fascism (CARF) (2002) 'Community Cohesion: Blunkett's new race doctrine'. *CARF 67*, London, CARF at http://www.carf.demon.co.uk/feat56.html accessed 31 August, 2009

Campbell, A (1984) *Girls in the Gang*. New York: Basil Blackwell

Cantle, T (2001) *Community Cohesion*. London: Home Office

Carrington, B (1998) 'Football's coming home – but who's home?, in A Brown (Ed) *Fanatics*. London: Routledge

Carter, H (2001) Riot trigger attack on pensioner was not racial. *Guardian Unlimited*, 20 September at http://www.guardian.co.uk/racism/ Story/0,2763,554719, 00.html

Centre for Contemporary Cultural Studies (CCCS) (1982) *The Empire Strikes Back*. London: Hutchinson

Cesari, J (2007) Ethnicity, Islam, and les banlieues: Confusing the Issues'. Social Science Research Council.http://riotsfrance.ssrc.org/Cesari/

Cheong, P, Edwards, R, Gouldbourne, H, Solomos, J (2007) Immigration, social cohesion and social capital: A critical review, *Critical Social Policy* (27)1:124-49

Choudhury, T (2007) *The Role of Muslim Identity Politics in Radicalisation: a study in progress*. Communities and Local Government, available at Http://www.communities.gov.uk/documents/communities/pdf/452628.pdf

Cohen, P (1996) Homing devices, in Amit-Talai, V and Knowles, C (Eds) *Re-situating identities: the politics of race, ethnicity and culture*, 68-82

Cohen, P and Bains, H (Eds) (1988) *Multiracist Britain*. London: Macmillan

Cohen, P (2003) Mods and Shockers: youth cultural studies in Britain, in A Bennett (ed) *Youth Research in Britain*. London: Sage

Cohen, S (2002) *Folk Devils and Moral Panics*. London: Routledge

Community Relations Commission (CRC) (1976) *Between Two Cultures*. London: CRC

Connell, R (1987) *Gender and Power*. Stanford, Stanford University Press

Connell, R (1995) *Masculinities*. Berkeley. University of California Press

Connell, R (1996) Teaching the boys: new research on masculinity, and gender strategies for schools. *Teachers College Record*. 99: 206-235

Connell, R (2005). Growing up masculine: Rethinking the significance of adolescence in the making of masculinities. *Irish Journal of Sociology* 14(2), 11-28

Connolly, C (1991) Washing our linen: one year of Women Against Fundamentalism. *Feminist Review* 37:68-77

Connolly, P (1998) *Racism, Gender Identities and Schooling*, London, Routledge

Cornish, P (2008) Terrorism, radicalisation and the Internet. Report of a private round-table discussion meeting, London: Chatham House 31 July available at http://www.chathamhouse.org.uk/files/12134_0708terrorism_internet.pdf

Corrigan, P (1976) Doing nothing, in S Hall and T Jefferson (Eds) *Resistance Through Rituals*, London: Hutchinson

CRE (2003) Briefing 307, London: Commission for Racial Equality

Crick, B (1998) *Education for Citizenship and the Teaching of Democracy in Schools*, London: Qualifications and Curriculum Authority

Cunningham, S and Lavellete, M (2004) Active Citizens or irresponsible truants? School Student Strikes Against the War. *Critical Social Policy* 24(2):255-269

Daley, J (2008) White working class boys need structure and competition to succeed *Telegraph*.co.uk 16 December available at structurehttp://blogs.telegraph.co.uk/news/janetdaley/5983638/White_working_class_boys_need_structure_and_competition_to_succeed/ accessed 10 January, 2009

Davies, B (1989) *Frogs and Snails and Feminist Tales. Preschool Children and Gender* (pp.1-152). Sydney: Allen and Unwin.

Davies, B and Harre, R (1991) Positioning: the discursive production of selves, *Journal for the Theory of Behaviour,* 20(1): 44-63

DCLG (2009a) *The Turkish and Turkish Cypriot community in England: understanding Muslim ethnic communities.* London: Department for Communities and Local Government

DCLG (2009b) *The Afgham Muslim Community in England: understanding Muslim ethnic communities.* London: Department for Communities and Local Government

DCSF (2009) *Deprivation and Education: the evidence on pupils in England, foundation stage to key stage 4.* London: Department for Children, Schools and Families

Deakin, N (1970) *Colour, Citizenship and British Society,* London, Panther Books

Delamont, S (2000) The anomalous beasts: hooligans and the history of sociology of education. *Sociology* 34(1):95-111

Denham, J. (2002) *Building Cohesive Communities: A Report of the Ministerial Group on Public Order and Community Cohesion.* London: Home Office

Denham, J (2009) Speech at the National Prevent Conference, Birmingham, 8 December

DfEE (1997) *Excellence in Schools.* London: Department for Education and Employment

DfES (2001) *Schools Building on Success: Raising Standards, Promoting Diversity, Achieving Results.* London: Department for Education and Skills

DfES (2007a) *Gender and Education: The Evidence on Pupils in England Research Information.* London: Department for Children, Schools and Families

DfES (2007b) *Diversity and Citizenship Curriculum Review.* London: Department for Children Schools and Families

DIUS (2007) *Promoting good campus relations, fostering shared values and preventing violent extremism in the name of Islam in universities,* London: Department for Innovation, Universities and Skills

Dodd, D (1978) Police and thieves on the streets of Brixton. *New Society,* 16 March

Dodd, V (2006) Universities urged to spy on Muslim students. *Guardian,* 16 October

Dodd, V (2009) Anti-terror code would alienate most Muslims. *Guardian,* 17 February

Donald, J and Rattansi, A (1992) (Eds) *'Race', Culture and Difference.* London: Open University in association with Sage

Dwyer, C (Ed) (1999) Veiled meanings: British Muslim women and the negotiation of differences. *Gender, Place and Culture* 6(1):5-26

Dwyer, C (2000) Negotiating diasporic identities: young British South Asian Muslim women. *Women's Studies International Forum* 23(4):475-486

Eade, J (1990) Nationalism and the Quest for Authenticity: The Bangladeshis in Tower Hamlets. *New Community* 16(4):493-503

Eade, J (1994) Identity, Nation and Religion: Educated young Bangladeshi Muslims in London'. *International Sociology* 9(3):77-94

Earle, R and Phillips, C (2009) Con-Viviality: Identity Dynamics in a Young Mens' Prison, in M. Wetherell (Ed) *Liveable Lives: Negotiating Identities in New Times.* Basingstoke: Palgrave

Enneli, P, Modood, T and Bradley, H (2005) Young Turks and Kurds: A set of invisible disadvantaged groups. York: Joseph Rowntree Foundation

Epstein, D, Elwood, J, Hey, V, Maw, J (1998) (Eds) *Failing Boys? Issues in Gender and Achievement.* Buckingham: Open University Press.

Flynn, D (2003) Tough as old boots? Asylum, Immigration and the paradox of New Labour Policy, a discussion paper, London: Joint Council for Welfare of Immigrants (JCWI)

Forgacs, D (1988) *A Gramsci Reader.* London: Lawrence and Wishart

Francis, B (2002) Is the future really female? The impact and implications of gender for 14-16year olds' career choices. *Journal of Education and Work*, 15(1):75-88

Francis, B and Skelton, C (2001) Men teachers and the construction of heterosexual masculinity in the classroom, *Sex Education*, 1, pp. 9-21.

Frosch, S, Phoenix, A, and Pattman, R (2002) *Young Masculinities: Understanding Boys in Contemporary Society*, Bastingstoke:Palgrave

Fryer, P (1985) *Staying Power: The History of Black People in Britain*, London, Pluto Press

Fryer, P (1988) *Black People in the British Empire: An Introduction*, London, Pluto

Fuller, M (1980) Black girls in a London comprehensive school, in R Deem (Ed) *Schooling For Women's Work.* London: Routledge and Kegan Paul

Fuller, M (1982) Young female and black, in B Troyna and R Hatcher, *Black Youth in Crisis.* London: Allen and Unwin

Fuller, M (1983) 'Qualified criticism, critical qualifications', in L Barton and S Walker (Eds) *Race, Class and Education.* London: Croom Helm

Garland, D (1996) The limits of the sovereign state: strategies of crime control in contemporary society, *British Journal of Criminology*, 36(4):445-471

Garland, D (2008) On the Concept of Moral Panic. *Crime Media Culture* 4:9-30

Gewirtz, D (1991) Analyses of racism and sexism in education and strategies for change. *British Journal of Sociology of Education*, 12 (2):183-201

Gewirtz, S (1998) Post-welfarist schooling: a social justice audit. *Education and Social Justice* 1 (1):52-64

Gewirtz, S (2001) *The Managerial School: Post-welfarism and Social Justice in Education.* London: Routledge

Giddens, A (1991) *Modernity and Self-Identity: Self and Society in the Late Modern Age.* Cambridge: Polity Press

Gill, D, Mayor, B and Blair, M (1992) *Racism and Education.* London: Open University in association with Sage

Gillborn, D (1997) Young black and failed by school: the market, education reform and black students. *Journal of Inclusive Education* 1(1):65-87

Gillborn, D (2006) Citizenship Education and Placebo: 'standards', institutional racism and education policy. *Journal of Education, Citizenship and Social Justice* 1(1):83-104

Gillborn, D (2008) *Racism and Education: coincidence or conspiracy*. London: Routledge

Gillborn, D (2009) Education: the numbers game and the construction of White Racial Victimhood, in K Sveinsson (Ed), *Who cares about the white working class*. London: Runneymede

Gillborn, D and Youdell, D (2000) *Rationing Education: policy, practice, reform and equity.* Buckingham: Open University Press

Gilroy, P (1982) Police and thieves, in Centre for Contemporary Cultural Studies (CCCS) *The Empire Strikes Back.* London: Hutchinson

Gilroy, P (1987) *There Ain't No Black in the Union Jack: The Cultural Politics of Race and Nation.* London: Hutchinson

Gilroy, P (2004) *The End of Multiculturalism* Gilroy, P (2004) *After Empire: Multiculture or Postcolonial Melancholia,* London: Routledge

Gilroy, P and Lawrence, E (1988) Two-tone Britain: white and black youth and the politics of anti-racism, in P Cohen and H Bains (Eds), *Multi-Racist Britain.* London: MacMillan

Giroux, H (1983) Ideology, agency and the process of schooling, in L Barton and S Walker (Eds) *Social Crisis and Educational Research.* London: Croom Helm

Glees, A and Pope, C (2005) *When Students Turn to Terror: terrorist and extremist acativity on British campuses.* London: The Social Affairs Unit

Glynn, S (2002) Bengali Muslims: the new East End radicals? *Ethnic and Racial Studies* 25:6:969-988

Gokay, B (2009) Tectonic shifts and systemic faultlines: a global perspective to understand the 2008-9 world economic crisis, *Alternatives: Turkish Journal of International Relations* 8(1) 29-35

Goldberg, D (1990) *Anatomy of Racism.* Minneapolis: University of Minnesota Press

Gowan, P (2009) Crisis in the heartland, consequences of the new wall street system, *New Left Review*, 55: Available at http://newleftreview.org/?page=article&view=2759 last accessed 30 August, 2010

Gramsci, A (1971) *The Prison Notebooks.* London: Lawrence and Wishart

Griffin, C (1993) *Representations of Youth,* Cambridge, Polity Press

Griffin, C (1985) *Typical Girls? Young Women from School to the Job Market*, London: Routledge and Kegan Paul

Griffin, C (1986) Black and white youth in a declining job market: unemployment amongst Asian, Afro Caribbean and White young people in Leicester, Centre For Mass Communications Research, Leicester University Research Report Series

Grosvenor, I (1997) *Assimilating Identities: racism and educational policy in post 1945 Britain.* London: Lawrence and Wishart

Gutzmore, C (1983) Capital, 'Black youth' and crime, *Race and Class* xxv(2):13-30

Hall, S (1980) Race, articulation and societies structured in dominance, in *Sociological Trends: Race and Colonialism.* Paris: UNESCO

Hall, S (1988) *The Hard Road to Renewal: Thatcherism and the Crisis of the Left.* London: Verso

Hall, S (1990) Cultural, Identity and Diaspora, in J Rutherford (Ed) I*dentity, Culture, Community, Difference.* London: Lawrence and Wishart

Hall, S (1992) New ethnicities, in J Donald and A Rattansi (Eds), *Race, Culture, Difference.* London: Open University in association with Sage

Hall, S and Jefferson, T (Eds) (1976) *Resistance Through Rituals.* London: Hutchinson

Hall, S, Critcher, C, Jefferson, T, Clark, J and Roberts, B (1978) *Policing the Crisis: Mugging, the State and Law and Order.* London: Macmillan

Hargreaves, J (1990) Urban dance-styles and self-identities: The specific case of Bhangra. Sport: *Kultur Veranderung* (19):146-160

Harris, P (2001) Fears of racial time-bomb in riot-hit towns, *Guardian Unlimited* Sunday August 5 at http://www.guardian.co.uk/racism/Story/0,2763,53249,00.html

Harvey, D (2003) *The New Imperialism.* Oxford: Oxford University Press

Haw, K (1994) Muslim Girls' Schools: a conflict of interests? *Gender and Education* 6(1):63-76

Hebdige, D (1979) *Subculture: the meaning of style.* London: Routledge

Heidensohn, F (1985) *Women and Crime.* London: Macmillan

Hesse, B. (ed) (2000) *Un/settled Multiculturalisms: Diasporas, Entanglements, Transruptions.* London: Zed Books

Hillyard, P (1993) *Suspect Community: people's experiences of the prevention of terrorism act in Britain.* London: Pluto Press

Hoberman, J (1986) *The Olympic Crisis: Sport, Politics, and the Moral Order.* New York: Aristide D. Caratzas

Home Office (2001) *Community Cohesion: A Report of Independent Review Team led by Ted Cantle.* London, The Stationery Office

Home Office (2005) Preventing violent extremism working group reports: August-September 2006. London: The Stationery Office

Home Office (2006) *Countering International Terrorism: The United Kingdom's strategy,* London: The Stationery Office

Home Office (2009) *Pursue prevent Protect Prepare: the United kingdom's strategy for countering international terrorism.* London: The Stationery Office

Hopkins, P (2006) Youthful Muslim masculinities: gender and generational relations. Transactions of the *Institute of British Geographers* 31(3):337-352

Hopkins, P (2007) Global events, national politics, local lives: young Muslim men. *Environment and Planning* 39:1119 -1133

Huntingdon, S (1997) *The Clash of Civilizations and the remaking of world order.* New York: Simon & Schuster

Jackson, C, Paechter, C and Renold, E (2010) *Girls and Education:3-16: Continuing Concerns, New Agendas.* Maidenhead: Open University Press

Jackson, R, Gunning, J, Breen Smyth, M (2007) The case of critical terrorism studies. Paper presented at the 2007 annual meeting of the American Political Science Association, 30 August

Jarvie, G (1990) (Ed) *Sport, racism and ethnicity.* London: Falmer Press

Jefferson, T (2008) Policing the crisis revisited: The state, masculinity, fear of crime and racism. *Crime Media Culture* 4(1):113-121

Jessop, B (1990) *State theory: putting the capitalist state in its place.* Cambridge: Polity

Jessop, B (2003) 'From Thatcherism to New Labour: neo-liberalism, workfarism and labour market regulation' in H Overbeek, (Ed) *The Political Economy of European Unemployment: European integration and the transnationalization of the employment question.* London: Routledge.

Jones, K (2009) The dynamic relationship between knowledge, identities, communities and culture, http://beyondcurrenthorizons.org.uk/thedynamic-relationship-between-knowledge-identities-communties-and-culure/ accessed 30 August, 2009

Kabbani, R (1989) *Letter to Christendom.* London: Virago

Kalra, V. (2002) Extended review-riots, race and reports: Denham, Cantle, Oldham and Burnley inquiries. In National Youth Agency (Ed) *Promoting Community Cohesion and the Young: a report of the forum meeting of 25 June 2002*, Leicester, National Youth Agency.

Kearney, M (2005a) No 'UK apology' for colonial past. *BBC News*, 15 January

Kearney, M (2005b) Brown seeks out 'British values'. *BBC News*, 14 March

Kenny, A (1999) What happened to antiracist education?' *Education and Social Justice* 1(3): 2-4

Kerbaj, R (2009) Muslim population 'rising 10 times faster than rest of society. *The Times*, 30 January

Kerr, M (1958) *The People of Ship Street.* London: Routledge and Kegan Paul

Kessler, S, Ashendon, D J, Connell, RW, and Dowsett, GW (1985) Gender Relations in secondary schooling. *Sociology of Education* 58:34-48

Khan, V S (1976) Pakistani women in Britain. *New Community* 5 (1-2):99-108

Khan, V S (1977) The Pakistanis, in J L Watson (Ed) *Between Two Cultures.* Oxford: Basil Blackwell

Klug, F (1989) Oh to be in England: the British case study, in F Anthias and N Yuval Davis (Eds). *Woman, Nation, State.* London: Macmillan

Knott, K and Khoker, S (1993) Religious and ethnic identity among young Muslim women in Bradford. *New Community* 19(4):593-610

Kreikenbaum, M (2010) The Lies of Thilo Sarrazin. *World Socialist Website*, 28 September http://wsws.org/articles/2010/sep2010/sarr-s28.shtml accessed 29 September, 2010

Kundnandi, A (2002) The death of multiculturalism, Institute for Race Relations 1 April 2002 http://www.irr.org.uk/2002/april/ak000001.htmlce accessed 15 July, 2010

Kundnani, A (2007) *The end of tolerance, Racism in 21st Century Britain.* London: Pluto

Kundnani, A (2009) *Spooked: how not to prevent violent extremism.* London: Institute of Race Relations

Lawrence, E (1982) Just plain common sense: the roots of racism, in Centre for Contemporary Cultural Studies (CCCS) *The Empire Strikes Back.* London: Hutchinson

Layton-Henry, Z (1992) *The Politics of Immigration.* Oxford: Blackwell

Lees, S (1997) *Ruling Passions: Sexual Violence, Reputation and the Law.* Buckingham: Open University Press

Lee, S (2006) Gordon Brown and the 'British way'. *The Political Quarterly* 77(3):326-378

Leonard, E (1987) *Women, Crime and Society.* London: Longman

Leppard, D and Fielding, N (2005) 'The Hate' reported in the *Sunday Times*, July 10

Mac an Ghaill (1994) *The Making of Men.* Buckingham: Open University Press

Mac An Ghaill, M (1992) 'Coming of age in the 1980's England: reconceptualising black students' schooling experience, in D Gill *et al* (Eds), *Racism and Education.* London: Sage in association with the Open University

Mac an Ghaill, M (1994) Beyond the white norm: the use of qualitative methods in the study of black youths' education, in P Woods and M Hammersley (Eds), *Gender and Ethnicity and Schools*

Mac an Ghaill, M (1988) *Young, Gifted and Black: Student-Teacher Relations in the Schooling of Black Youth.* Milton Keynes: Open University Press

MacClancy, J (1996) *Sport, Identity and Ethnicity.* Oxford: Berg

MacDonald, R and Marsh, J (2005) *Disconnected Youth? Growing Up in Britain's Poor Neighbourhoods.* Basingstoke: Palgrave Macmillan

Macpherson, W (1999) *The Stephen Lawrence Inquiry Report.* London: The Stationery Office

MacRobbie, A (1991) *Feminism and Youth Culture: From Jackie to Just Seventeen.* London: Macmillan

MacRobbie, A and Garber, J (1975) 'Girls and subcultures', in S Hall and T Jefferson (Eds), *Resistance Through Rituals: Youth Subcultures in Post-war Britain*

Mahony, P and Hextall, I (2000) *Reconstructing Teaching: Standards, Performance and Accountability.* London: Routledge Falmer

Malik, K (1989) The Rushdie affair: The 'sleeping demons' awake. *Living Marxism*, (May):24-27

Mani, L and Frankenburg, R (1993) 'Cross currents, crosstalk: race, 'postcoloniality' and the politics of location'. *Cultural Studies*, 7(2):292-400

Martino, W (1999) 'Cool boys', 'party animals', 'squids' and 'poofters': Interrogating the dynamics and politics of adolescent masculinities in school. *The British Journal of the Sociology of Education* 20 (2): 239-263

Martino, W and Pallotta-Chiarolli, M (2003) *So what's a boy? Addressing issues of masculinity and schooling.* Maidenhead, UK: Open University Press

Maughan Brown, D (2007) Disingenuous, patronising and dangerous. *Education Guardian*, 19 February

Mays, J (1954) *Juvenile Delinquency.* London: Jonathan Cape

McDowell, L (2002) Masculine discourses and dissonances: Strutting 'lads', protest masculinity and domestic respectability. *Environment and Planning: Society and Space*, 20:97-119

McGhee, D (2003) Moving to 'our' common ground – a critical examination of community cohesion discourse in twenty-first century Britain. *Sociological Review* 51(3): 376-404

McGhee, D (2008) *The End of multiculturalism? Terrorism, Integration and Human rights.* Buckingham: Open University Press

Miles, R (1982) *Racism and Migrant Labour.* London: Routledge and Kegan Paul

Milne, S (2010a) This tide of anti-Muslim hatred is a threat to us all. *Guardian*, 25 February

Milne, S (2010b) This attempt to rehabilitate empire is a recipe for conflict. *Guardian*, 10 June

Mirza, H S (1992) *Young, Female and Black.* London: Routledge

Mirza, K (1989) The silent cry: second generation Bradford Muslim women speak, *Muslims in Europe* 43, Centre for the study of Islam and Christian-Muslim Relations

Modood, T (1988) Black racial equality and Asian identity. *New Community* 2(3):397-404

Modood, T (1992) British Asian Muslims and the Rushdie affair, in J. Donald and A Rattansi (Eds) *Race, Culture, Difference,* London: Open University Press in association with Sage

Modood, T (2006) Ethnicity, Muslims and Higher Education entry in Britain, *Teaching in Higher Education*, 11(2):247-250

Muir, T and Wetherell, M (2010) *Identity, Politics and Public Policy.* London: IPPR

Mulgan, G and Wilkinson, H (1997) 'Freedom's children and the rise of generational politics', in G. Mulgan (Eds) *Life after Politics: New Thinking for the Twenty First Century.* London: Fontana

Mulhern, F (2000) *Culture/Metaculture.* London: Routledge

Naber, N (2005) Muslim First, Arab Second: A Strategic Politics of Race and Gender. *Muslim World*, 95: 479-495

Nayak, A (2003) *Race, Place and Globalisation.* Oxford: Berg

Nayak, A and Kehily, M J (1996) Playing it straight: masculinities, homophobias and schooling. *Journal of Gender Studies,* 5: 211-230.

Ofsted (1999) *Raising the Attainment of Minority Ethnic Pupils: School and LEA Responses.* London: Office for Standards in Education

ONS (2006) *Social Trends.* London:Office for National Statistics

Open Society Institute (2002) *Monitoring Minority Protection in the EU: The Situation of Muslims in the UK.* Budapest: Open Society Institute

Osler, A (2009) Patriotism, multiculturalism and belonging: political discourse and the teaching of history. *Educational Review,* 61(1) 85-100

Osler, A (2010) Patriotism, citizenship and political discourses and the citizenship curriculum, in Grimmit, M (Ed) *Religious education and social and community cohesion: challenges and Opportunities.* Southend on Sea: McCrimmons

Ousley, H (2001) *Community Pride not Prejudice: making diversity work in Bradford.* Bradford: Bradford Vision.

Ozga, J (1999) Two nations? education and social inclusion-exclusion in Scotland and England. *Education and Social Justice* 1 (3): 44-50

Pantazis, C and Pemberton, S (2009) From the 'old' to the 'new' suspect community, Examining the impacts of recent UK counter terrorist legislation. *British Journal of Criminology,* 49:646-666

Parker-Jenkins, M (1994) Islam shows its diverse identities, *Times Educational Supplement* 21 October

Parsons, T (2009) 'Come off it Amir Khan – what are you moaning about?' *Mirror Sport,* 12 December http://www.mirror.co.uk/sport/more-sport/boxing/2009/12/12/come-off-it-amir-khan-what-are-you-moaning-about-115875-21891065/ accessed 20 January, 2010

Peach, C. (2005) Britain's Muslim Population: An Overview, in T Abbas, (Ed) *Muslim Britain: Communities under Pressure.* London: Zed Books

Pearson, G (1976) 'Paki-Bashing' in a North East Lancashire Cotton Town: A case study and its history' in G Mungham and G Pearson (Eds) *Working Class Youth Culture.* Routledge and Kegan Paul: London

Pearson, G (1983) *Hooligan: a history of respectable fears.* Basingstoke: Macmillan

Phillips, T (2005) After 7/7: Sleepwalking into segregation. Speech given at Manchester Council for Community Relations, 22 September

Poynting, S (2006) What caused the Cronulla riot? *Race and Class* 48(1) 85-92

Qureshi, K (2004) Respected and Respectable: The Centrality of Performance and 'Audiences' in the (Re)production and Potential Revision of Gendered Ethnicities, *Particip@tions,* 1(2), May Available at http://www.participations.org/volume%201/issue%202/1_02_qureshi_article.htm

Ramamurthy, A (2006) The politics of Britain's Asian youth movements'. *Race and Class* 48(2)38-60

Ramji, H. (2007) Dynamics of Religion and Gender amongst Young British Muslims, *Sociology*, 12 (41)1171-1189

Rattansi, A (2004) New Labour, new assimilationism. *Open Democracy*, 6 October

Reay, D (2001) Finding or losing yourself? Working class relationships to education. *Journal of Education Policy* 16(4):333-346

Reay, D (2008) 'Tony Blair, the promotion of the 'active' educational citizen, and middle-class hegemony'. *Oxford Review of Education*, 34(6):639-650

Reay, D, David, M and Ball, S (2001) Making a Difference?: Institutional Habituses and Higher Education Choice. *Sociological Research Online*, 5(4) <http://www.socres online.org.uk/5/4/reay.html

Reay, D, Hollingworth, S, Williams, K, Crozier, G, Jamieson, F, James, D and Beedell, P (2007) A Darker Shade of Pale?' Whiteness, the Middle Classes and Multi-Ethnic Inner City Schooling. *Sociology* (41):1041

Renold, E (2001) Learning the 'Hard' Way: boys, hegemonic masculinity and the negotiation of learner identities in the primary school'. *British Journal of Sociology of Education*, 22 (3):39-385

Renold, E (2005) *Girls, Boys and Junior Sexualities: exploring children's gender and sexual relations in the primary school.* London: RoutledgeFalmer

Rhodes, J (2009) Revisiting the 2001 Riots: New Labour and the Rise of 'Colour Blind Racism', *Sociological Research Online* 14(5)3 http://www.socresonline.org.uk/14/5/3. html

Rose, E J B, Deakin, N, Abrahams, M, Jackson, V, Peston, M, Vanags, A H, Cohen, B, Gaistkill, J and Ward P (1969) *Colour and Citizenship.* London: Oxford University Press for the Institute of Race Relations

Rose, N (1996) *Inventing Our Selves: Psychology, Power and Personhood.* New York: Cambridge

Runnymede Trust (1993) Growing gap between ethnic minority groups. *Runnymede Trust Bulletin* (265):4-5

Rutherford, J (Ed) (1990) *Identity, Community, Culture, Difference.* London: Lawrence and Wishart

Saeed, A, Blain, N and Forbes, D (1999) New Ethnic and National Questions in Scotland: post-British identities among Glasgow Pakistani teenagers. *Ethnic and Racial Studies*, 22(5):821-844

Saghal, G and Yuval-Davis, N (1992) *Refusing Holy Orders.* London: Virago

Samad, Y (2004) Muslim Youth in Britain: ethnic to religious identity, International Conference Muslim Youth in Europe. Typologies of Religious Belonging, Turin Edoardo Agnelli centre for Comparative Religious Studies, 11 June

Samad, Y (1992) Book burning and race relations: political mobilisation of Bradford Muslims, *New Community* 18(4):507-19

Samad, Y (1998) Media and Muslim Identity: Intersections of Generation and Gender. Special Issue on Muslims in Europe, *Innovation: European Journal of Social Science*, 10(4): 281-282

Sarrazin, T (2010) Deutschland schafft sich ab: Wie wir unser Land aufs Spiel setzen, *Deutsche Verlags-Anstalt* 30 Aug 2010

Scarman, (1982) *The Scarman Report: The Brixton Disorders, 10-12 April 1981*, London: Penguin Books

Schilling, C (2004) Physical capital and situated action: a new direction for corporeal sociology. *British Journal of Sociology of Education* 25(3): 473-487

Scraton, P (1987) (Ed) *Law, Order and the Authoritarian State*. Buckingham: Open university Press

Searle, C (1993) Race before wicket, empire and the white rose, *Race and Class* 32(3)31-48

Sewell, T (1998) *Black Masculinities and Schooling: How Black Boys Survive Modern Schooling*. Stoke-on-Trent, Trentham Books

Shah, R (1992) *The Silent Minority: Children With Disabilities in Asian Families*. London: National Children's Bureau

Shain, F (2003) *The Schooling and Identity of Asian Girls*, Stoke-on-Trent: Trentham Books

Shain, F (2009) Uneasy Alliances: Muslims and communists. *Journal of Communist Studies and Transnational Politics* 25(1):95-109

Shain, F (2010) Refusing to integrate: Asian girls and achievement, in C Jackson, C Paechter, and E Renold, (Eds) *Girls and Education 3-16: continuing concerns, new agendas.* Maidenhead: Open University/McGraw Hill

Siddiqui, H (1991) Winning freedoms, *Feminist Review* 37:18-20

Sivanandan, A (1982) *A Different Hunger*. London: Pluto Press

Sivanandan, A (1983) From resistance to rebellion: Asian and Afro-Caribbean struggles in Britain. *Race and Class* 23 (2\3):111-52

Sivanandan, A (2000) UK: reclaiming the struggle. *Race and Class* 42(2):67-73

Skeggs, B. (2004) *Class, Self, Culture*. London: Routledge

Skelton, C. (2001) *Schooling the Boys: masculinities and primary education*. Buckingham: Open University Press

Skelton, T and Valentine, G (1998) *Cool Places: geographies of youth cultures*. London: Routledge

Sky News (2008) Muslims Back Amir after Radical's Rant. *Sky News*, March 25

Smart, C (1976) *Women, Crime and Criminology*. London: Routledge and Kegan Paul

Solomos, J (1992) The politics of immigration since 1945, in P Braham, A Rattansi, and R Skellington (Eds). *Racism and Anti Racism*. London: Open University in association with Sage

Solomos, J and Back, L (1994) Conceptualising racisms: social theory, politics and research. *Sociology* 28(1):143-161

Southall Black Sisters (1990) *Against the Grain: A Celebration of Survival and Struggle*. London: Southall Black Sisters

Spalek, B (2007) Disconnection and exclusion: pathways to radicalisation? In T Abbas (Ed) *Islamic Political Radicalism: a European perspective.* Edinburgh: Edinburgh University Press

Spalek, B El Awa, S, McDonald L and Lambert, R (2008) *Police-Muslim Engagement and Partnerships for the Purposes of Counter-Terrorism: an examination.* Birmingham: University of Birmingham

Spinley, M (1953) *The Deprived and the Privileged.* London: Routledge and Kegan Paul

Sprott, W J, Jephcott, P and Carter, M (1954) *The Social Background of Delinquency,* Nottingham, University of Nottingham Press

Swain, J (2002) 'The Resources and Strategies Boys Use to Establish Status in a Junior School without Competitive Sport'. *Discourse: Studies in the Cultural Politics of Education* 23 (1): 91-107

Taylor, M (1985) *The Best of Both Worlds.* Oxford: NFER

Thomas, K (1990) *Gender and Subject in Higher Education.* Buckingham: Open University Press

Thorne, B. (1993) *Gender Play: Girls and Boys in School.* New Brunswick: NJ, Rutgers

Tomlinson, S (1983) 'Black women in higher education – case studies of university women in Britain' in L Barton and S Walker (Eds), *Race, Class and Education.* London: Croom Helm

Tomlinson, S (2008) *Race and Education: Policy and Politics in Education.* Maidenhead: Open University Press

Travis, A (2009a) Two thirds of UK terror suspects released without charge. *Guardian,* 13 May

Travis, A (2009b) New plan to tackle violent extremism, *Guardian,* 3 June

Wacquant, L (2008) *Urban Outcasts: A comparative Sociology of Advanced Marginality.* Cambridge: Polity Press

Ware, V (1992) *Beyond the Pale: White Women, Racism and History.* London:Verso

Watson, J (1977) (Ed) *Between Two Cultures: Migrants and Minorities in Britain.* Oxford: Basil Blackwell

Webster, C. (2003) Race, space and fear: imagined geographies of racism, crime, violence and disorder in Northern England. *Capital and Class* 80:63-90

Weiner, G (1985) (Ed) *Just A Bunch of Girls.* Milton Keynes: Open University Press

Werbner, P. (1996) Fun Spaces: On Identity and Social Empowerment among. British Pakistanis, *Theory, Culture and Society* 13(4): 53-79

Werbner, P (2002) *Imagined Diasporas Among Manchester Muslims: The Public Performance of Pakistani Transnational Identity Politics.* London: James Currey

Werbner P (2007) Veiled Interventions in Pure Space: Honour, Shame and Embodied Struggles among Muslims in Britain and France. *Theory, Culture and Society,* 24(2): 161-187

REFERENCES

Werbner P.(2005) Islamophobia: Incitement to Religious Hatred – Legislating for a New Fear? *Anthropology Today,* 21(5):5-9

Westwood, S (1990) 'Racism, black masculinity and the politics of space' in J Morgan and D Hearn (Eds) *Men and Masculinities and Social Theory.* London: Unwin Hyman

Whitty, G (1998) 'New Labour, education and disadvantage', *Education and Social Justice* 1(1):2-8

Whitty, G (2008) Evaluating Blair's education legacy: some comments on the special issues of Oxford Review of Education, published in *Oxford Review of Education*, 35(2): 267-280

Williams, J (2000) Asians, Cricket and Ethnic Relations in Northern England. *Sporting Tradition*, 16 (2): 39-53

Williams, R (1980) 'Base and superstructure in Marxist cultural theory' in R. Williams (Ed) *Problems in Materialism and Culture.* London: New Left Books

Willis, P (1977) *Learning to Labour: How Working Class Kids Get Working Class Jobs.* Farnborough: Saxon House

Willis, P (1990) *Common Culture.* Milton Keynes: Open University Press

Willis, Paul (2003). Foot Soldiers of Modernity: The Dialectics of Cultural Consumption and the 21st-Century School. *Harvard Educational Review* 73(3):390-415

Wilson, A (2006) *Dreams, Questions, Struggles: South Asian Women in Britain.* London: Pluto Press

Women Against Fundamentalism (WAF) (1991) *Newsletter* No.1

Worley, C (2005) 'It's not about race. It's about the community': New Labour and 'community cohesion'. *Critical Social Policy* 25(4):483-496

Youdell, D. (2003) Identity Traps or How Black students fail: the interactions between biographical, sub-cultural and learner identities. *British Journal of Sociology of Education* 24(1):3-20

Youdell, D. (2006) *Impossible Bodies, Impossible Selves: exclusions and student subjectivities.* London: Springer

Yuval Davies N (1992) 'Fundamentalism, Multiculturalism and women in Britain', in J Donald and A Rattansi (Eds) *Race, Culture, and Difference.* London: Sage in association with the Open University

Zizek, S (2010) 'Liberal Multiculturalism masks an old barbarism with a human face'. *Guardian*, 3 October

Index